A Short History of America

Coen Nishiumi

Level 5

IBC パブリッシング

はじめに

　ラダーシリーズは、「はしご (ladder)」を使って一歩一歩上を目指すように、学習者の実力に合わせ、無理なくステップアップできるよう開発された英文リーダーのシリーズです。

　リーディング力をつけるためには、繰り返したくさん読むこと、いわゆる「多読」がもっとも効果的な学習法であると言われています。多読では、「1. 速く 2. 訳さず英語のまま 3. なるべく辞書を使わず」に読むことが大切です。スピードを計るなど、速く読むよう心がけましょう（たとえば TOEIC® テストの音声スピードはおよそ 1 分間に 150 語です）。そして 1 語ずつ訳すのではなく、英語を英語のまま理解するくせをつけるようにします。こうして読み続けるうちに語感がついてきて、だんだんと英語が理解できるようになるのです。まずは、ラダーシリーズの中からあなたのレベルに合った本を選び、少しずつ英文に慣れ親しんでください。たくさんの本を手にとるうちに、英文書がすらすら読めるようになってくるはずです。

《本シリーズの特徴》
- 中学校レベルから中級者レベルまで5段階に分かれています。自分に合ったレベルからスタートしてください。
- クラシックから現代文学、ノンフィクション、ビジネスと幅広いジャンルを扱っています。あなたの興味に合わせてタイトルを選べます。
- 巻末のワードリストで、いつでもどこでも単語の意味を確認できます。レベル1、2では、文中の全ての単語が、レベル3以上は中学校レベル外の単語が掲載されています。
- カバーにヘッドホーンマークのついているタイトルは、オーディオ・サポートがあります。ウェブから購入／ダウンロードし、リスニング教材としても併用できます。

《使用語彙について》
レベル1：中学校で学習する単語約1000語

レベル2：レベル1の単語＋使用頻度の高い単語約300語

レベル3：レベル1の単語＋使用頻度の高い単語約600語

レベル4：レベル1の単語＋使用頻度の高い単語約1000語

レベル5：語彙制限なし

CONTENTS

| Chapter 1 |
European Settlement and the Colonial Period 1

| Chapter 2 |
The American Revolution 17

| Chapter 3 |
The Building of the New Nation 29

| Chapter 4 |
The Civil War 53

| Chapter 5 |
Reconstruction and the Settlement of the West 65

| Chapter 6 |
World War I and American Prosperity 77

| Chapter 7 |
America in the World 89

Epilogue 117

Word List 120

Chapter 1

European Settlement and the Colonial Period

第1章

広大な森と草原、そして険しい山と砂漠。そこには農耕や狩猟をしながら生活をする先住民がいました。そんな広大なアメリカという土地に、忽然と現れたヨーロッパの帆船。15世紀から17世紀にかけて、宗教の自由、そして新たな富を求めて多くの人が、新大陸に渡ってきました。数ヶ月をかけた航海の末、アメリカの東海岸にたどり着いた人々は、そこで少しずつ町をつくり、農地を開墾します。彼らの多くはイギリスやオランダなどからのプロテスタントでした。勤勉で信仰のあつい彼らこそ、今のアメリカの土台をつくった人々だったのです。

第1章で使われている用語です。わからない語は巻末のワードリストで確認しましょう。

- ☐ claim
- ☐ confederation
- ☐ constitution
- ☐ cultivation
- ☐ deport
- ☐ fort
- ☐ persecution
- ☐ restrict
- ☐ ritual
- ☐ settle
- ☐ smuggling
- ☐ succession

THE EARLIEST BEGINNINGS

People say that America is a young country. However, before the Europeans came, it was the home of the American Indian, or Native American. Various Indian tribes were scattered all over the American continent. It is said they came to America during the ice age, when Eurasia and America were connected by land where the Bering Strait now lies between Alaska and Russia.

Their arrival took place between 30,000 and 15,000 years ago. Recently many ruins and archeological evidence have been discovered that shows how they lived and practiced religious rituals. Even before 2,000 years ago many American Indians harvested squash, corn, pumpkins, and other crops. And before 800 years ago this agricultural technology was well developed.

Iroquois women doing agricultural work

Iroquois Five Nations, c.1650

Around that time there were many villages and even towns all over the continent. However, the lives of the American Indians changed drastically when Europeans discovered America and started to settle in their territories.

ERA OF EUROPEAN SETTLEMENT

Many people believe that it was Christopher Columbus who discovered America. However, hundreds of years before Columbus, some Europeans had already been to North America, but for various reasons they didn't settle there. Most European sailors were afraid of the Atlantic Ocean and did not sail west. It was at the end of the 15th century that European explorers officially "discovered" the New World, as North and South America were called.

Before the 15th century European explorers did not expect to find a new continent. They just wanted to do business in the Indies, which was the name for India and all of Southeast Asia then. Trading in the Indies and Asia could make people very rich. However, the Ottoman Empire captured Constantinople in 1453 and blocked the land and sea routes between Europe and the East. So the traders had to find new routes. First, Portuguese sailors sailed south along the African continent. They managed to reach India

Chapter 1 European Settlement and the Colonial Period

in this way, but it took too long. Then, some sailors began to believe that they could reach India by traveling across the Atlantic.

Europeans became less afraid of the Atlantic Ocean during the Renaissance period when scientists began to say that the world was round. If that was true, then it should be possible to get to India by traveling west.

So, with support from Spain, Columbus set sail in search of the Indies in 1492. He went west and finally found several islands. As already mentioned, he believed he had reached the Indies in the east. However, the islands he saw were actually in the west, so they became known as the West Indies. Columbus and other explorers later found the North and South American continents, but Columbus seems to have believed until his death that the land

The landing of Columbus

A Short History of America

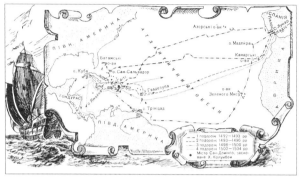

The voyages of Christopher Columbus

he found was part of Asia. The name "America" comes from the name of the Italian sailor Amerigo Vespucci. He was the first explorer to claim that the new land was a new continent.

Spain explored this New World for many years. In 1513 Vasco Núñez de Balboa crossed the Isthmus of Panama and discovered the Pacific Ocean. Hernán Cortés destroyed the Aztec empire in Mexico. Hernando de Soto explored the area from Florida to the lower Mississippi between 1539 and 1542. They took gold and silver from the American Indians by force. In those early days, although they did not intend to build colonies, the Spanish claimed that the land was theirs.

However, in Europe, England became powerful

and defeated the Spanish Armada in 1588. After that, Spain was no longer very active in the northern part of the New World, and more British people settled in North America. In the meantime, the Frenchman Jacques Cartier explored the Saint Lawrence River in Canada. France claimed the lands around the river as well as the valley of the Mississippi.

The French who settled in America were mainly businesspeople and priests. Robert de La Salle, who used to be a member of the Society of Jesus, explored the Great Lakes region and the Mississippi River, and in 1682 he named the Mississippi River region Louisiana in honor of the French king Louis XIV.

While the British and French became active in North America, Spain continued to rule most of Central and South America. Most these Latin American countries became independent in the first half of the 19th century, after a series of revolutions.

LIFE AND CONFLICT AMONG PROTESTANTS

The history of the United States of America begins with the English colonies that were established on the Atlantic coast of North America from Florida to New Hampshire. Dutch, French, and Swedes also went to live in North America. For example,

French settled in Carolina, and Swedes settled along Delaware River.

In 1497 John Cabot became the first Englishman to reach the New World. When England started to have fierce conflicts with Spain in the 16th century, the English became more interested in the New World as a way of weakening their rival. Sir Walter Raleigh tried to set up colonies in North America between 1583 and 1587. He failed, but later many other English people followed his example and immigrated to the New World.

After the long trip across the Atlantic Ocean, sailors would shout with joy when they saw the silhouette of the continent far ahead over the waves. Their diaries said when the new continent got closer, the sweet smell of soil and plants reached the boat, a wonderful change after they had spent so many days exposed to waves and salty breezes.

England wanted to colonize America for several reasons. First, they learned how the Spanish had become rich by trading

Portrait of Sir Walter Raleigh, who set up the first colony in North America (1598)

with the New World. They went to the New World in the hope of making a fortune. Second, many of them went to North America to escape religious persecution. In England the official church was the Protestant Anglican Church. Other Protestants, non-Anglicans, Jews, and Catholics were poorly treated, so some of them decided to leave England for the New World. The New World offered them shelter and the chance of a fresh start.

The first permanent English settlement in North America was Jamestown in Virginia, which was

Embarkation of the Pilgrims

The first Thanksgiving at Plymouth

established in 1607. The town was named after King James I of England, who supported the explorers. Captain John Smith played an essential role in the establishment of this settlement and other English colonies. Later, Maryland, which is named after the wife of King James, was founded in 1632. In 1620 a group of Puritans (English Protestants) called the Pilgrims left England in a ship called the *Mayflower* and landed in Massachusetts. They founded the colony of Plymouth, which grew slowly.

On the other hand, Dutch people settled in what is now New York. Almost all of them were Protestants. The settlement was founded in 1609 by Henry Hudson who came to Manhattan. He was British, but he was an employee of the Dutch West India Company. New York became the colony under the Netherlands in 1626 and was named New

Henry Hudson's *Half Moon* sailing ship

Amsterdam. Around that time, there were 1,500 people living in New York. A fort and a windmill were located at the southern tip of Manhattan. To protect themselves from attackers, they built a wooden wall on the outskirts of town. The famous Wall St. was named after it. In 1664, however, the British took control of New Amsterdam by threatening it with gunboats, eventually changing its name to New York.

In this way, the New World became the home of many Protestants. However, they did not always live together harmoniously. Conflicts arose related to their beliefs. For example, a Puritan leader named Anne Hutchinson who insisted on the equality between man and women was deported from the Massachusetts Bay Colony. Roger Williams, who was

William Penn, founder of Pennsylvania (1681)

also a Puritan and asked for the freedom of religious belief, was forced to leave the Massachusetts colony after a series of political struggles. In 1636 he founded an open community that welcomed people of all religions. This community later became Rhode Island. These concepts of freedom of belief and speech became essential parts of colonial culture in the future movement toward American independence.

Many more settlements were set up at various places. People who left Massachusetts for religious reasons built new communities in New Hampshire and Maine. Most of these so-called New England colonies joined together to fight against American Indians and the Dutch. They called their group the New England Confederation.

Colonization continued after 1660. For example, an Englishman named William Penn, who was a

The famous Zenger trial

Quaker, came to America because he sought freedom of belief. He founded Pennsylvania in 1681. The English claimed the area along the Atlantic coast from Maine to Carolina. Georgia was also founded by English people. Florida, however, was still under the rule of Spain.

THE DEVELOPMENT OF THE COLONIES

The people who went to America had a variety of political and religious ideas. As England did little to help the English people living in the New World, the early settlers decided to rule themselves. So, in order to govern each village and town, they established their own laws and rules. For example, in 1619 they formed the Virginia House of Burgesses, which was the first law-making body in America. In 1620 the Pilgrims agreed to the Mayflower Compact on their way to America, and they promised to follow the laws set by the majority. In 1639 the settlers on the Connecticut River produced the Fundamental Orders, the first written constitution in America. New England saw the growth of direct democracy. Then the freedom of the press was established. A printer and publisher named Peter Zenger was found innocent in court after being arrested for criticizing the governor of New York.

The battle of Quebec, fought on December 31, 1775

Still, many people could not vote or work in the new government; only the rich who were religious and socially or morally "good" could take part in politics.

On the surface, it seemed that the New World was independent from Europe. However, when war occurred in Europe, the flames quickly leaped across the Atlantic. The English colonies had wars with the French from 1689 to 1697. It was called King William's War. In the same period, people in Europe were fighting in the War of Spanish Succession from 1701 to 1713.

When Britain was involved in the Seven Years War in Europe and fought against France, they fought in North America, too. In 1755 the French and Indian War between England and France broke out in North America. Some French-Canadian forts and Quebec were captured by the English. As

Chapter 1 European Settlement and the Colonial Period

a result, the French colony of Louisiana was handed over to Spain.

France lost nearly all of its land in North America. Most of Canada and the islands of the West Indies became English. The English colonies continued to fight the Native Americans, who were unable to unite under a single strong leader. They gradually fell under the rule of the Europeans.

By 1760 there were nearly 1.5 million Europeans in America, and their life was very similar to that in England. There were two main social classes: the rich and the poor. Some people in the wealthy class were already rich when they arrived in America and came to increase their fortune, while others joined the wealthy class by investing in real estate.

On the other hand, poor people had to work hard to pay back the money they had borrowed to travel to America. There were also many black slaves. Black slaves were captured and brought from Africa. It was the dark side of American history. Many of them were cruelly treated as laborers on tobacco and rice plantations. They were sold and bought like commodities.

Life was not easy for the colonists. The roads were terrible, and travel was difficult, especially in bad weather. The forest was deep. In summertime, travelers were bothered by mosquitos and wild animals. In winter, a terribly cold wind bit their faces. They farmed land, created villages, and sometimes traded with American Indians and sold what they received or produced to Europe. For example, in the early days many New York immigrants went out into the wilderness to hunt beavers since its fur was used to make hats in Europe.

Generally, most people did agricultural work after preparing their land for cultivation. They produced and exported wood, flour, potatoes, rice, indigo, pork, beef, and fish. But they bought sugar from the West Indies. The South also exported tobacco all over the world.

There were no factories, so business people took the raw material to the homes of workers, who made products like shoes, fabric, and nails. Products of better quality had to be imported from Europe. England restricted business and factory operations in America because it was afraid of competition. It controlled the trade of the American colonies and made them pay substantial taxes. So the colonists turned to smuggling. This led to the independence movement of the 1770s.

Chapter 2

The American Revolution

第 2 章

アメリカは、ヨーロッパから移住してきた人々によって開墾されていきます。そんなとき、ヨーロッパではフランスやイギリスなど、大国がそれぞれの覇権をめぐって戦争を繰り返していました。その戦火はアメリカにも飛び火します。先住民のアメリカンインディアンをも巻き込んだ戦争の末、宗主国のイギリスは植民地の人々に戦争でかかった費用を税金として課していきます。これがアメリカに住む人々の怒りとなったのです。アメリカはついに独立への道を選択します。東部13州がイギリスに対して立ち上がった独立戦争。厳しい戦いの末、1783年についにアメリカ合衆国が成立したのです。

第 2 章で使われている用語です。わからない語は巻末のワードリストで確認しましょう。

- ☐ assertive
- ☐ autonomy
- ☐ convince
- ☐ declaration
- ☐ delegate
- ☐ deletion
- ☐ impose
- ☐ massacre
- ☐ mercenary
- ☐ representation
- ☐ treason
- ☐ tyranny

FRUSTRATION AND BEGINNINGS OF THE REVOLUTION

In the 18th century the colonists began to stand up against British rule. Many preferred autonomy rather than following British rules and regulations, particularly the tax system.

But at first, the colonists did not work all together. Some were angry at the British government, but many still wanted the British to rule North America. Some colonists supported the British king and others had connections with the British government and businesses. However, to cover the cost of the French and Indian War, the British tried to make the American colonies pay more taxes between 1760 and 1775, and this made more colonists angry.

In 1764 the English king, George III, set up new trade limits and taxes. The British government said that the money from these taxes was needed to defend the American colonies, but the colonists thought that the money might be used to weaken their independence.

The British also established a new law, the Stamp Act of 1765, which put a tax on all printed material produced in the colonies. This was more money that the colonists had to pay to the government.

"Taxation without representation is tyranny" was a famous phrase of an American politician, James Otis. He said that the colonists did not have to pay taxes because they were not represented in the British government. His phrase soon became a slogan that was used to show how angry the colonists were about the taxes.

Over the years, the anger of the colonists continued to grow. At the Virginia Assembly, the Virginian lawyer Patrick Henry even said, "Give me liberty, or give me death." This famous statement encouraged people who wanted independence. When someone cried "Treason!" Henry famously replied, "If this is treason, make the most of it." His words affected the people who were angry like him, and they formed a new group called the "Sons of Liberty."

These actions led England to end the Stamp Act, but it was not a victory for the colonists. New laws called the Townshend Acts were created shortly afterward, and new taxes were placed on imported goods.

At the same time, England tried to suppress the colonists' protests, and the British army led by General Thomas Gage arrived in Boston in 1770.

The soldiers shot into an angry crowd and killed five people. This event was later named the Boston Massacre. Because of the Boston Massacre, important Bostonians like the politicians Samuel Adams and John Hancock led further public protests against British rule.

To calm the anger of the colonists, the British minister Lord North canceled the Townshend Acts, but he continued to put a small tax on tea. For the colonists, however, the problem was no longer the amount of taxes but the idea of taxation itself. So this small tax on tea only added to their anger.

During the Boston Tea Party on December 16, 1773, Samuel Adams and other Bostonians dressed as Native Americans, boarded a British ship, and threw its boxes of tea into Boston Harbor. George III was upset by these events, and in 1774 he tried to

Boston Tea Party (1773)

impose new strict measures, including the closing of Boston Harbor. The colonists had to decide if they could successfully fight against superior British power. They decided to risk it. In September 1774, representatives from the colonies held the First Continental Congress. All the colonies except Georgia chose to fight Britain for independence. Georgia did not take part because its economy was wholly depended on the British.

In April 1775 the British army marched to Concord, northwest of Boston, to seize the colonists' weapons that were stored in warehouses there. Learning of this, the colonists gathered together and fought the British at Lexington. They didn't win, but the colonists in Concord succeeded in driving the British back to Boston.

These battles were the beginning of the American Revolutionary War, also known as the American War of Independence, which lasted from 1775 to 1783. Massachusetts and parts of New England now celebrate the 19th of April as Patriots' Day to remember the events at Lexington and Concord.

THE REVOLUTIONARY WAR FOR INDEPENDENCE

As the colonists became more assertive, all the efforts to reach an agreement between the Whigs

Chapter 2 The American Revolution

(rebels) and the British Parliament failed. The thirteen colonies formed the Continental Army and fought battles not only in Lexington, but also in Fort Ticonderoga and Bunker Hill, and later in Falmouth and Maine. The Continental Army even attempted to invade Quebec in Canada to capture the British colony there, but failed.

The thirteen colonies held the Second Continental Congress in May 1775. This time Georgia sent a representative. The Congress was responsible for military operations until 1781, and it appointed George Washington of Virginia as the Commanding General. People in the South greatly respected and supported him as a war hero and a large landowner.

In 1776 the colonists became more convinced

United States Declaration of Independence, ratified in 1776

that independence should be their final goal when they read Thomas Paine's pamphlet *Common Sense*. The same year, Thomas Jefferson wrote a draft of the Declaration of Independence. The document was signed by several state delegates and passed Congress on July 4, 1776. But it took weeks for all the representatives to sign the document. All of the states joined the first Union of States between 1777 and 1781.

The delegates promised to follow the principles of the Declaration of Independence, which stated that "all men are created equal" and had the right to "life, liberty and the pursuit of happiness." It also noted that the people had the right to change or remove governments that did not continue to give them these rights. The Declaration was a blueprint for American freedom and democracy and also served as a slogan for opposition to Great Britain.

It is important to point out that Thomas Jefferson originally included in the Declaration the statement that all slaves should be freed. This seemed the right thing to do if "all men are created equal." However, Southern landowners could not survive without slaves, so they insisted that the statement be removed. As a result, in order to keep the colonies united, the "Founding Fathers of the United States,"

Chapter 2 The American Revolution

Signing of the Declaration of Independence

including Washington and John Adams, had to agree to its deletion. Slaves fought bravely in the war in the hope of becoming free, but most of them did not win their freedom. Some slaves also fought for Britain.

Fighting continued in the North. General Howe of the British forces left Boston and tried to capture New York. General Washington resisted, but the British army defeated the Americans in the Battle of Long Island in August 1776. Washington and his men were forced to retreat to New Jersey. However, between December 1776 and January 1777, Washington's army was victorious in Trenton and Princeton, But General Howe defeated Washington again and captured Philadelphia, which was then the capital of America. Next, Washington led his troops to Valley Forge, north of Philadelphia, for the winter of 1777. In that winter 2,500 American soldiers died of disease and the cold weather.

In Canada the American troops were more successful with the help of various foreign mercenaries. One of them was Marquis de La Fayette. He met Benjamin Franklin in Paris. Franklin was one of the major activists of the American Revolution. When the war against the British broke out, he went to France to seek support from the French government. La Fayette was deeply impressed by Franklin's thought and ideals. La Fayette decided to help American troops.

Another example was Casimir Pulaski, who was an officer from the Polish-Lithuanian Commonwealth. He was forced into exile due to the oppression of the Russian Empire and came to Paris. It was Marquis de La Fayette who asked him to help the Americans.

Due to the struggle for power in Europe, France wanted to see England fail in America. After the American troops defeated the British army at Saratoga, north of New York, in October of 1777, France decided to support America. In 1778 America and

Chapter 2 The American Revolution

Washington leading his troops to Valley Forge

Battle of Lexington and Concord, 1775

France became allies. This gave rise to new problems between France and England, but it was an excellent outcome for the American side.

From 1778 to 1781 no significant victories were claimed by either side. In the meantime, however, Spain and the Netherlands decided to support America, and many European volunteer soldiers came to help America. Britain was almost alone, so George III finally gave up trying to make the Americans agree to British rule. In the summer of

Washington crossing the Delaware

1783, a formal peace treaty was negotiated, and the American colonies gained independence. The first capital of this new nation was New York City.

The new republic now consisted of thirteen states. It was quite large. Its western border was the Mississippi River, and its southern boundary was the Gulf of Mexico, though Florida, which was in the south, still belonged to Spain.

Chapter 3

The Building of the New Nation

第3章

ヨーロッパからの移民によって作られたアメリカ。しかし、それは各地に移住してきた人々の自治によって成り立つ共同体のようなものでした。独立したアメリカは、強い政府によって統率しようとする人々と、それぞれの町や村、そして州の自治を尊重するべきだとする人々が激しく論争を繰り返します。この論争こそ、現在のアメリカにも受け継がれている、連邦政府と州との関係の原点となるのです。そして、そんな論争を経ながらも、アメリカは国家として成長をはじめたのです。アメリカは東海岸一帯から内陸に向けて領土を拡大していきます。テキサスを併合し、西部の未開の地にも多くの人が足を踏み入れました。未開の新大陸は、次第にアメリカの広大な領土へと変貌を遂げていったのです。

第3章で使われている用語です。わからない語は巻末のワードリストで確認しましょう。

- [ ] amendment
- [ ] annexation
- [ ] compromise
- [ ] deploy
- [ ] discrimination
- [ ] doctrine
- [ ] expertise
- [ ] federal
- [ ] prominent
- [ ] property
- [ ] unanimous
- [ ] unprecedented

THE STRUGGLE TO CREATE A NEW NATION

Now that the war had ended, the thirteen states became more interested in their own problems. They did not want to create a central, federal government right away, although they knew they would eventually need one.

A temporary central government had been established in 1777. It loosely held the states together during the war, but each state still enjoyed its own freedom and independence. However, after the war there were disadvantages to not having a central government. For example, in some cases soldiers were not paid for their service. Further, the paper money printed by the Continental Congress was almost worthless and caused confusion. Even after the war the British duties on American exports to Britain remained high, but without a central government America had no power to resist them.

Flag of the United States (1777–1795)

The states realized they needed a strong central or federal government to solve these problems. But their efforts to increase federal power often failed because any changes required a unanimous vote, a vote in which all states gave their agreement. However, it was finally decided to hold a Constitutional Convention in Philadelphia in 1787. At this convention Benjamin Franklin, Gouverneur Morris, and Alexander Hamilton began drafting a constitution.

The Constitution was not immediately approved by the thirteen states. Some of the states were afraid that they would lose power. It took three years for all of them to agree. The first state to approve the Constitution was Delaware on December 7, 1787, and the last was Rhode Island in 1790. This debate over the needs of central government and the freedom of the states still remains one of the major political issues of the United States.

The Constitution of the United States provides guidance to the U.S. federal government on how the government should be run, how politicians should be elected and what they should and shouldn't do. The Constitution also contains essential rules for the selection of officials by Congress, religious freedom, freedom of speech, freedom of the press, and the education of its people.

Consequently, the United States of America became a democratic nation. However, it was a democracy only for white males who owned property. No women, native Americans, or non-white people had the right to vote or could run for Congress. In other words, the Constitution was only the beginning of a long road to real democracy in which all people could participate.

THE FIRST ADMINISTRATIONS AND THEIR DEVELOPMENT

In 1789 George Washington was elected the first president of the United States, and John Adams became the first vice president. George Washington was popular because of his excellent leadership in the Revolutionary War. In the same year the first Congress was also elected.

The first federal government faced a variety of unprecedented issues since there was no other republican government in the world to serve as a model.

George Washington, the first president of the United States

Europe was very curious about this new republic. Some nations saw America as an example of how to establish a republican type of government which did not exist in Europe at that time, except in Switzerland.

The first Secretary of State was Thomas Jefferson, and the first Secretary of the Treasury was Alexander Hamilton. Using his financial expertise, Hamilton suggested that the country pay its debts by taxing its citizens and persuaded the federal government to be responsible for all the states' debts. The first national bank was established in 1791 while Hamilton was Secretary.

While Washington was president, Congress agreed to ten amendments to the Constitution, which are known as the Bill of Rights because they describe the rights of citizens. Three new states joined the republic in the 1790s: Vermont in 1791,

Left:
Thomas Jefferson
Right:
Alexander Hamilton

Chapter 3 The Building of the New Nation

The Bill of Rights

The fourth president of the United States, James Madison, primary author of the Bill of Rights

Kentucky in 1792, and Tennessee in 1796.

Around the same time, political parties were established based on differences of opinion about how to run the country. The Federalist Party, led by Alexander Hamilton, believed in a centralized federal government, while the Democratic-Republican Party, led by Thomas Jefferson, believed in giving more power to the states. George Washington belonged to the Federalist Party. He was re-elected president in 1793 for the second time, despite opposition from his own party.

Washington did not want to be president for a third time, even though he was still popular and could have won, so in 1797 John Adams, the man whom Washington wanted to be president, was

A Short History of America

The capital of the United States in 1800, city of Washington

elected as the second president of the United States, while Thomas Jefferson became vice president.

Before he retired, Washington gave a famous farewell speech. In this speech he talked about the importance of federalism and the Constitution and suggested that America should not get involved in any wars in Europe, but should remain neutral. Since then, this has been the basic diplomatic policy of the United States.

Washington, D.C., which was founded in 1790, was named after President Washington. It was established on the Potomac River between Maryland and Virginia and became the capital of the United States in 1800, one year after Washington's death.

THE EARLY PROGRESS OF DEMOCRACY

John Adams's presidency (1797–1801) took place at the same time as Napoleon Bonaparte's rise to power

Chapter 3 The Building of the New Nation

in France. Following the suggestion in Washington's speech, the United States stayed neutral during the war in Europe between France and Britain.

This angered France, and the two countries came into conflict. Adams wanted to negotiate with France and settled the issue peacefully, but the Federalist Party disagreed and stopped supporting him. Partly because of this, Adams lost the 1801 election to Democratic-Republican Thomas Jefferson, who then became the third president. Adams is the only president to be defeated by his own vice president. One of Jefferson's goals was to increase the size of the United States.

In 1800 Napoleon had secretly bought the Louisiana Territory in the southern part of North America from Spain. This meant that the farmers in the west could no longer send their farm products to the east of the country. They were furious, and some of them even wanted to go to war with France.

Jefferson's solution was to offer to buy the Territory from France. To his surprise, Napoleon agreed since he needed the money in France's war against Britain. In 1803 Napoleon sold Louisiana to the United States for only 15 million dollars. This purchase doubled the size of the United States and added rich lands to the nation. The purchase also made it possible to expand the nation to the west since Americans could now travel freely up and down the length of the Mississippi River.

At this time the United States was trading profitably with both Britain and France, but trade was getting difficult because of the increasing tensions in Europe. Then, in 1806, Napoleon prevented all commercial ships from entering British ports. Britain did the same. As a result, American ships could not visit British or French ports any longer. To trade with one of these countries, America had to oppose the other. This made it difficult for the United States to remain neutral.

In 1809 the fourth president of the United States, James Madison, was elected. Around the same time the British government declared that American sailors were still British subjects and forced them to work on British ships. This angered the United States and was seen as a cause for war. At the same time, America wanted to expand the size of the country to the west and to the north into Canada. Canada was then ruled by Britain, and the Native Americans who had fought against America were supported by Britain. So many Americans came to believe that it was time to fight against Britain.

Madison declared war against Great Britain in

Chapter 3 The Building of the New Nation

June 1812. The Federalist Party opposed this decision, which made the party unpopular after the war. Later in 1812, Madison was re-elected president.

THE WAR OF 1812 AND THE GROWTH OF THE UNITED STATES

Although the American army failed to win in Canada, it won victories at sea. The warship *USS Constitution* (also known as *Old Ironsides*) was extraordinarily successful. The Americans also won a battle on Lake Erie and took control of the Great Lakes. They sometimes used American Indians to fight on their side. American troops successfully defeated the American Indians fighting on the British side and continued to expand the area they controlled. However, the British in Canada hit back at the United States and occupied Washington for a period of time. The winning and losing of battles

The battle of Queenston Heights, 1812

Andrew Jackson leads the defense during the Battle of New Orleans, 1815

continued for a number of years. Both American and British sides were exhausted. A peace treaty called the Treaty of Ghent was signed in December 1814.

However, the news did not reach America in time to avoid a battle at New Orleans in January 1815. The U.S. Army led by Andrew Jackson won a great victory in this battle, and the Americans wrongly believed that they had won the war against Britain. Andrew Jackson became a war hero, and he was later elected president.

Having experienced war, the United States turned once more to expansion and development. Also, more immigrants were arriving in the country. At the same time, the U.S. government had to pay an enormous war debt. The Southern plantations were suffering because they could not trade with Great Britain, but manufacturing was developing in the North.

Chapter 3 The Building of the New Nation

In 1816 James Monroe was elected president. At that time, the differences between the North and the South were growing more prominent. For example, Northeastern manufacturers now needed the government to tax imports to protect their products, but the Southern states had a different view. The South wanted free trade on an international level. Their plantations produced cheap raw materials, and they had to export them to make money.

The Northern and Southern states had different systems. The North were the free states without slavery. The South's economy depended on slavery. They were divided along the Mason-Dixon line, which ran between Maryland and Pennsylvania, based on a survey by Charles Mason and Jeremiah Dixon in 1763–67.

Indiana became a state in 1816 and Mississippi in 1817. Around that time, the steamboat had come into

The Erie Canal, connecting the Hudson River and Lake Erie

operation thanks to Robert Fulton. This new means of transportation helped develop the western part of the nation. Better roads were also being built all over the country. To deal with the increase in inland traffic, the Erie Canal was constructed connecting the Hudson River and Lake Erie. It was 360 miles long. With its completion in 1825, western products could be quickly brought to New York for export. A postal system was also developed, though it was very expensive.

The territory of the United States kept expanding. Spain did not make an effort to keep Florida, so the United States bought the area in 1821 for only $5 million. In 1820 Monroe was elected president again. In 1823, during his second term as president, he established the Monroe Doctrine. This doctrine was against more colonization of the Americas by European countries and against America getting involved in wars in Europe. Instead, the United States wanted to protect Central and South America and put them under American influence to maintain its interests. Great Britain supported this policy.

It was 1818 when the Missouri Territory expressed a wish to join the United States. Since it insisted on having slavery, this made the relationship between the North and South much worse. The North wanted

Chapter 3 The Building of the New Nation

to prevent the spread of slavery, but the South wanted to expand slavery and the plantation system. Admission of Missouri was strongly opposed, but eventually Congress approved it with a compromise. The compromise involved various conditions, including the admission of Maine as a free state and a ban on slavery to the north of the Missouri border.

In 1824 John Quincy Adams, son of the second president John Adams, became president. In this election many states introduced the current voting system in which ordinary citizens choose representatives (electors) who select the president. This is called the Electoral College.

Adams ran for president against William Harris Crawford, Henry Clay, and Andrew Jackson, who had many supporters in the South. Because none of them received enough votes to be the winner, the House of Representatives made the final decision. Adams was selected. Clay became Secretary of State, and rumor suggested that Adams and Clay had made a secret deal, with Clay becoming Secretary in return for his support of Adams in the final decision-making process.

In 1828 Adams introduced high taxes on imports, which angered the Southern states, especially South Carolina.

There was much political confusion during Adams's presidency, and the political parties were reorganized. The Federalist Party had already disappeared in 1820. The Democratic-Republican Party broke apart. Adams and his party established the National Republican Party in 1824, and Andrew Jackson and his followers formed the Democratic Party in 1828.

In the presidential election of 1828, Adams was defeated by Andrew Jackson. Those who opposed Jackson created the Whig Party in 1833 under the leadership of Henry Clay. The Whigs disagreed with the expansion of the country to the west and supported industrial development in the North.

THE RISE OF THE WEST AND THE PROBLEM OF TEXAS

Andrew Jackson was from a poor farming family in the South. He worked hard to promote democracy with the support of poor laborers and pioneers. As a result, all of the states gave all white men the right to vote during his presidency. This was called Jacksonian Democracy. On the other hand, he did not believe in having a national bank, which at this time was called the Second National Bank of the United States, and he tried to close it down.

Chapter 3 The Building of the New Nation

In addition, when he was president, there was a spoils system, which is also known as a patronage system. In this system, civil service positions were given to the supporters of the winning political party. Sometimes people were not qualified, and this caused problems.

Also, some states challenged the federal government, claiming that they had the right to change a federal law if they believed it was against the Constitution. For example, in 1832, Jackson lowered the rate of the import taxes set by Adams in 1828, but South Carolina was still not happy about this. So it decided that the federal import taxes of 1828 and 1832 were unconstitutional and ignored them. Thus the tension between the North and South increased again.

In 1832, Jackson was elected to a second term as president. He closed down the Second National Bank even though the Supreme Court wanted to keep it. He also carried out various democratic reforms, including the organization of unions, free public schooling, and prison reform.

However, the discrimination against American Indians and black slaves still continued under his presidency. Sometimes slaves rebelled for freedom. When Nat Turner, who was a black slave in Virginia, revolted against plantation owners in 1831, many of his followers and innocent blacks were massacred. This was just one of many similar cases in that era.

This period also saw the start of the "golden age" of American literature with the publication of works by Nathaniel Hawthorne, Ralph Waldo Emerson, Edgar Allan Poe, and Henry Wadsworth Longfellow.

The presidential election of 1836 was won by the Democratic candidate Martin Van Buren. While he was president, the financial crisis called the Panic of 1837 occurred. The weak banking system and the powerless central bank made the situation worse. Many banks and enterprises failed.

However, the West was prospering despite the problems in Washington. Though the pioneers faced hardships, they continued to travel West through North America toward the Pacific Ocean. About this time, two more states were admitted to the United States, Arkansas in 1836 and Michigan in 1837. Two years before Michigan became a state, Texas gained its independence from Mexico.

Between 1810 and 1821, Mexico rebelled against Spain to gain its independence. During that chaotic period, many Americans migrated into Texas. When Mexico gained independence, the new government, which was not yet stable, saw this migration as a threat. In 1835, American settlers started fighting against Mexican soldiers deployed in Texas. After many fiercely fought battles, including the battle of the Alamo, Texas became independent in 1836. Samuel Houston, who led the war for independence, became the first president of the Republic of Texas.

When Vice President John Tyler became president due to the death of William Harrison in 1841, he tried not to get involved in party politics, especially concerning the annexation of Texas. Texas wanted to

The battle of the Alamo (February 23–March 6, 1836)

join the United States, but the Americans were worried that they would have to go to war with Mexico if Texas were admitted. Also, some European countries opposed the idea because they feared that America would become too big.

Tyler wanted to annex Texas but waited until he won the presidential election of 1844. The Democratic candidate, James K. Polk, supported Tyler, and Tyler tried to persuade Congress. Finally, Congress admitted Texas in 1845 along with Florida. Iowa joined in 1846.

In 1845 the columnist John L. O'Sullivan described America's expansion to the West as its "manifest destiny." He said that God had given the United States a mission to expand throughout the whole of North America. This slogan was frequently used to justify America's efforts to expand its territory.

THE MEXICAN WAR AND SOCIAL AND ECONOMIC DEVELOPMENTS

Mexican President Santa Anna was furious about losing Texas and was ready to fight the United States. But he was thrown out of office, and an immediate battle was avoided.

However, there was still significant disagreement

CHAPTER 3 THE BUILDING OF THE NEW NATION

between Mexico and Texas. Texans believed that its southwestern border was the Rio Grande River, but the Mexican government claimed that it was the Nueces River. The American government sent an army to the Rio Grande River and fought the Mexicans. In 1846 Congress declared that Mexico had started a war with the U.S.

In 1847 General Taylor entered Mexico. Though American forces were smaller in number, they defeated Mexico at Buena Vista. General Winfield Scott invaded Mexico via Vera Cruz and took Mexico City in September 1847.

Eventually, the two countries signed the Treaty of Guadalupe Hidalgo, and Mexico gave up all the lands north of the Rio Grande. After the war, the United States continued to take over huge areas of North America, which would later become the states of California, Nevada, Utah, Arizona, New Mexico, Colorado, and Wyoming.

Social advancements and cultural changes also occurred during this era. In farming, the iron plow had been developed and was in use in 1855, and the cotton gin had been used since 1793. In transportation, steamboats were being used more than ever before. Also, because knowledge of the weather was essential for travel by sea, the United States

Weather Bureau was established. On the other hand, technological advancement caused the extinction of certain animals and birds. Vast herds of buffalo used to roam across the land, but by this time their number had been greatly reduced.

The population of the country was not only growing, but many people were moving West. Particularly in the mid-19th century, to gain free land,

On the Oregon Trail across the continental divide by large-wheeled wagon

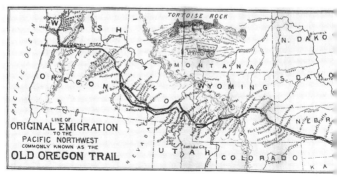

Chapter 3 The Building of the New Nation

many settlers moved from the East to the Oregon Territory, now the states of Oregon and Washington. It was a long and dangerous journey. They were often confronted by American Indians trying to protect their lands. This path to the Oregon Territory was called the Oregon Trail, and it became the symbol of manifest destiny.

In 1790 most people lived in rural areas in the East, and the population totaled about 4 million people. By 1860 the population had grown to 31 million, and many people were living in towns and cities so they could work in factories. Others were pursuing new opportunities in the vast wild lands of the West.

There were a great many social and technological developments in the 19th century. During the first

The Emigrant Trail route, connecting the Missouri River to valleys in Oregon

half of the 1800s, coal was used for heating and gas for lighting. And soon people were using iron stoves and matches. The telegraph came into operation in 1844, and just over a decade later the first transatlantic cable was laid. The Baltimore and Ohio Railroad also opened, and the printing press was improved.

Advertisement for the Baltimore and Ohio Railroad, 1864

There were also improvements in the educational system, including more opportunities for women. The nation's first women's college was Wesleyan Female College in Georgia, which was set up around 1836, and the first co-educational college, named Oberlin, was established in Ohio in 1833.

Chapter 4

The Civil War

第4章

アメリカは自由と平等、そして誰もが幸福を追求する権利があることを主張して、独立しました。しかし、そんなアメリカにはヨーロッパからの移民が経営する農場で働くアフリカから連れてこられた奴隷がいたのです。お金で売買され、人権も自由もなかった彼らの状況はひどいものでした。とくに南部では安価な労働力によって農業経営を支えていかなければならない経済的な事情もありました。そして、連邦政府は、南部の州のこうした事情にメスをいれることができなかったのです。そんな矛盾を解決しようと主張して、リンカーンが大統領に選ばれたとき、南部はアメリカ合衆国からの離脱を表明しました。奴隷制度の撤廃をスローガンに、連邦政府と南部諸州との内戦がはじまります。そして、アメリカの存亡をかけた大規模な内戦の結果、連邦政府が勝利したのでした。

第4章で使われている用語です。わからない語は巻末のワードリストで確認しましょう。

- ☐ abolish
- ☐ abolitionist
- ☐ conservative
- ☐ draft
- ☐ fugitive
- ☐ ironclad
- ☐ lynch
- ☐ preservation
- ☐ resentment
- ☐ riot
- ☐ uprising
- ☐ withdraw

THE DIVISION BETWEEN NORTH AND SOUTH

By mid 19th century the cities in the North controlled the U.S. economy. The South was still dependent on the conservative plantations. They needed cheap labor in the form of slaves. On the other hand, the abolitionists, who believed in freeing the slaves, increased in number in the North. They ignored the Fugitive Slave Act, which punished people if they protected runaway slaves, and helped slaves travel north to Canada through a secret network called the "underground railroad."

In the meantime, the United States acquired California as a result of the war with Mexico. Gold was discovered there in 1848, and thousands of people

Slave trading shop

Working California gold placer deposits, 1850

rushed to take advantage of this new opportunity. California quickly established a local government and applied for admission to the United States as a slave state.

This event further divided the North and South, one side calling for the end of the slave trade and the other calling for stricter fugitive slave laws. The disagreement between them was so serious that some states even considered leaving the United States. Congress met in December 1849, and Secretary of State Clay introduced a bill to prevent the United States from breaking up. The law was so full of compromise that it became known as the Omnibus Bill of 1850. In the bill, California would be admitted as a free state, and the slave trade was banned in Washington, D.C. On the other hand, slavery was not prohibited in the Territory of New

Scene from cotton plantation (1884)

Chapter 4 The Civil War

Mexico, and the Fugitive Slave Act was made stricter for the benefit of the South.

Throughout the 1850s slavery remained a significant issue. *Uncle Tom's Cabin* by Harriet Beecher Stowe, which was published in 1852, was very influential. It is probably the most famous anti-slavery novels in American history.

Cover of *Uncle Tom's Cabin*, first edition

The Kansas–Nebraska Act, drafted by Senator Stephen A. Douglas, was passed by Congress in 1854. The Act tried to settle the slavery issue in the Nebraska Territory by allowing each new state to decide if it wanted to be a slave state or a free state. Kansas voted against slavery, though it wasn't admitted as a state until 1861.

In 1856 James Buchanan of the Democratic Party was elected the 15th president. In this election the new Republican Party, which still exists today, appeared on the political scene.

The following year the Supreme Court ruling on the Dred Scott case shook the nation. Since Dred Scott once lived in Illinois and the Wisconsin Territory where slavery was illegal, he sued for his freedom. However, he lost his case in the Supreme Court. This case spread deep resentment among people who were against slavery.

During the presidential campaign of 1860, divisions within the Democratic Party and talk about the Southern states leaving the United States led to the victory of Abraham Lincoln of the Republican Party, even though none of the Southern states supported him. The South was starting to lose its influence as three more states became free states. Minnesota was admitted in 1858, Oregon in 1859 and Kansas in 1861. The Southern states became more and more dissatisfied.

THE CHAOS OF CIVIL WAR

By this time the idea of leaving the United States was not new. Some people said that just as the American colonies had left Great Britain, the Southern states had the same right to withdraw from the United States. South Carolina had wanted to break away for a long time, and after the Republican Party's victory in the presidential election of 1860, it decided to leave. Then Mississippi, Florida, Alabama, Georgia, Louisiana, and Texas followed.

Abraham Lincoln believed that all the states must remain as one nation. However, representatives from

Chapter 4 The Civil War

Abraham Lincoln (1863)

the seven separated Southern states met in Alabama and formed the Confederate States of America on February 4, 1861. Jefferson Davis (from Mississippi) became the president, and Alexander H. Stephens (from Georgia) became the vice president.

Lincoln stated in a speech that states could not leave the Union and the federal government had the power to enforce the preservation of the United States, which he called the Union. He also spoke of his desire for peace by saying, "We are not enemies, but friends. We must not be enemies." However, his wish did not come true.

The Battle of Fort Sumter in April 1861 marked

Confederate flag flying over Fort Sumter, 1861

the beginning of the American Civil War. Fort Sumter in South Carolina was attacked by Confederate forces, forcing the surrender of the Union troops. President Lincoln asked 75,000 men to join the Union army for a term of three months. This caused more Southern states to leave the Union.

The population of the North (21 million) was much larger than that of the South (nine million). Furthermore, one-third of the Southern population were slaves. The North also had greater material resources. However, the Southern Confederate states had more experienced military leaders. At first, Lincoln thought he could win quickly, but the fighting actually lasted for four years.

The first major battle took place at Bull Run, Virginia, in July 1861. The Union's 30,000 soldiers were defeated by a smaller Confederate force, with 3,000 men on the Union side being killed or wounded. The Union troops fled toward Washington. Lincoln called for an additional 50,000 volunteers.

The Union blocked off Southern ports to stop the Confederates from receiving foreign aid. It also attacked Richmond, the capital of Virginia. The Battle of Hampton Roads on March 8–9 in 1862 was the most significant sea battle of the Civil War. Though neither side was victorious, it would become

Chapter 4 The Civil War

famous as the first battle between ironclad ships.

The Confederates continued to fight well. General Robert E. Lee of the Virginian Army defended Richmond with 80,000 soldiers against General McClellan's 105,000 Union fighters. President Lincoln, once again, had to call for an additional 300,000 volunteers.

Ordinary citizens had to pay more taxes during the war because over $2 million was being spent every single day for military purposes. Meanwhile, Lincoln continued to lose thousands of soldiers, and General Lee was successful against the Union army.

After the Battle of Antietam on September 17, 1862, Lincoln stated that slaves in the Southern states would be freed if the Confederates did not return to the Union by January 1, 1863. Of course, the South did not respond, so he signed the Emancipation Proclamation (a presidential order to free the slaves) in 1863.

The war continued. The Battle of Gettysburg on July 1–3 in 1863 may be one of the most memorable battles of the Civil War. It lasted three days, resulting in the defeat of Lee's Confederate forces. Over 43,000 lost their lives.

It was a troubling time for all Americans. Soon after the Battle of Gettysburg, riots broke out in New

Crowd of citizens and soldiers with Lincoln at Gettysburg

General Ulysses S. Grant (1861)

General Robert E. Lee, the commander of the Confederate Army

York in protest against the draft. Angry mobs lynched blacks. The uprising was suppressed, but it shocked Union leaders.

After the Battle of Chickamauga in 1863, Ulysses S. Grant was appointed commander of the two divisions of the Union army; later he would become the Lieutenant General of the entire Union forces. Meanwhile, General Lee would become Commander-in-Chief of the Confederate troops in 1865.

Chapter 4 The Civil War

Fighting continued, mostly around Virginia and along the boundary between North and South. Lincoln was easily re-elected in 1864 for his second term as president. In the same year Nevada was admitted to the Union.

Then, in the spring of 1865, the Civil War came to an end. The North captured Richmond, and Lee surrendered to Grant at the Battle of Appomattox Court House on April 9, 1865.

The Civil War brought big changes to America. The cost of the war was huge—billions of dollars and over 800,000 deaths, leaving many in the South poor. It also changed politics and laws. The federal government was now superior to the states. Amendments to the Constitution abolished slavery and granted citizenship to blacks.

The Civil War also marked the beginning of modern warfare with advanced weapons that caused massive destruction and death. Unfortunately, the discrimination against blacks continued long after slavery was abolished. The damage in the relations between North and South would not be easily healed.

Chapter 5

Reconstruction and the Settlement of the West

第5章

南北戦争はアメリカに深い傷を残しました。南部は連邦政府の管理下におかれますが、再び国家が分裂しないように、連邦政府は次第に南部と妥協をしていきます。その結果、奴隷ではなくなったものの、アメリカにはその後長年にわたって黒人差別が横行するようになったのです。一方、アメリカは南北戦争を経て再び国家として統一されました。そして、西部の開拓が推し進められ、そこでのアメリカン・インディアンとの土地をめぐる争いも社会問題となりました。西海岸までアメリカが切り開かれ、鉄道によって東西が結ばれたとき、アメリカは強大な国家としていよいよ成長をはじめたのでした。

第5章で使われている用語です。わからない語は巻末のワードリストで確認しましょう。

- ☐ anti-trust
- ☐ corrupt
- ☐ depression
- ☐ diligent
- ☐ disaster
- ☐ fanatic
- ☐ ingenious
- ☐ outcome
- ☐ proactive
- ☐ reconciliation
- ☐ reconstruction
- ☐ segregate

THE RECONSTRUCTION PERIOD

Reconstruction is the name of the era from 1863 when the Emancipation Proclamation was announced to 1877.

On April 14, less than a week after Lee's surrender, President Lincoln was assassinated by a fanatic Confederate supporter. Vice President Andrew Johnson became president. He tried to follow Lincoln's broad-minded approach toward the South. But Congress was ruled by radical Republicans, who wanted to be stricter with the South and grant former slaves citizenship and the right to vote. It passed many laws to reconstruct the South and the nation: the Freedmen's Bureau Act to provide support to former slaves, the Civil Rights Bill to protect

Voting in New Orleans, 1867

the rights of former slaves, the Reconstruction Act to rule the South more strictly, and the Fourteenth Amendment so that blacks were classed as American citizens, and so on.

However, all the former Confederate states refused to accept the Fourteenth Amendment, which caused Congress to abolish the Southern state governments and put the Reconstruction Act into force. The government also put the South under the control of the U.S. army.

During the process of Reconstruction, however, Congress had to gradually compromise and return political power to the former Confederate states due to Southern resistance and to avoid the separation between the North and the South again.

After the period of Reconstruction, the wartime hero General Grant was the clear choice for president in the election of 1868. He entered presidential office at a time when the South was experiencing hard times—the radical Republicans had placed ever tighter controls on Southern whites. The white population could not accept the laws created during Reconstruction and instead created state and local laws (Jim Crow laws) to segregate blacks from white society. These laws remained valid until 1964 and were a source of racism in American culture.

Chapter 5 Reconstruction and the Settlement of the West

It was unfortunate that during Grant's administration, many of the supporters he appointed to government positions were corrupt, and government money was used for their own. Furthermore, several disasters hit America during his term. The Great Chicago Fire of 1871 was followed by the Great Boston Fire of 1872. Then there was financial panic when banks and businesses failed in 1873.

Around the same time, the government encouraged settlement in the West and dispatched the army to control the American Indians, whose lands and properties were in danger. Many Indian tribes made war against the U.S. government. However, they were gradually suppressed and forced to move to the places (reservations) that the government had reserved for them. Like blacks in the South, they had been segregated from general society.

In the election of 1876 Rutherford B. Hayes of the

Wounded Knee Massacre, U.S. soldiers putting Native Americans in grave (1891)

Republican Party ran against Samuel J. Tilden of the Democratic Party. Samuel Tilden got 500,000 more votes than Hayes but was still defeated. The results showed that the electoral system of selecting the president did not truly represent the will of the majority of voters. Even now, the president is elected by the electoral college, which is chosen by ordinary voters. The election results to choose the electoral college is called the popular vote. Unfortunately, even if a candidate for president receives more popular votes than other candidates, this does not mean he will receive the most electoral college votes. This happened in 2016 when Hilary Clinton received the most popular votes, but Donald Trump became president.

The election of 1876 was a similar case. However, the Democratic Party did not complain about the outcome. Many people suspected that a secret deal

Union Pacific Railroad connects the East and West

had been made with the Democrats and the South because President Hayes soon removed federal troops from the South and allowed the Southern states to govern themselves, which was what the Democratic Party wanted. It was the beginning of the reconciliation between the North and the South and the coming together as one nation.

In 1869 the East and West Coasts were finally connected by railroad. Many people went West to mine gold and silver. Agriculture became an essential part of Midwestern life. There were still vast uncultivated lands in the West, and many immigrants from Europe went to settle there, along with many new arrivals from China and Japan. It was mainly Chinese immigrants who helped to construct the transcontinental railroad.

However, a majority of the immigrants were working in the cities on the East Coast. The cities

Immigrants living on Mulberry Street, New York City, 1900

there were densely crowded. Most immigrants were poor but diligent, trying hard to support their families and their relations back in their mother countries.

Some successful immigrants invested their money in new ideas and businesses. Talented people made a fortune. Pushed by such immigrant power, the size of the American economy started expanding. And supported by such economic development, some ingenious people invented new technologies. The labor for such enterprises was supplied by these immigrants.

It was an age of invention and the railroad. Thomas Edison invented the phonograph, the long-lasting light bulb, the motion picture camera, and many other electronic devices. Alexander Graham Bell invented the telephone in 1876. Heavy industry like iron and steel production prospered. Andrew Carnegie made a fortune by making steel for railroads and buildings.

Thomas Edison, the inventor of many electrical devices

Gradually, America became one of the centers of commercial technology in the world.

POLITICAL ISSUES AND THE SPANISH–AMERICAN WAR

At first the U.S. government accepted silver and gold as legal money and allowed people to make coins freely, but as a government it needed to control the currency. In 1873 Congress passed the Coinage Act to stop the making of silver dollars. However, soon after, silver was discovered in the West, so mine owners fought for the removal of the Coinage Act. In 1878 the government promised to purchase silver to make coins, but this condition was removed in 1893.

Another hot topic in the 1890s was the need for an anti-trust law. The Sherman Anti-Trust Act of 1890 prohibited monopolies and restraints on trade.

While there is always a need for a stable economy, throughout history the economy has never remained the same, whether for investors, entrepreneurs, or bankers. The question is how the government can control economic conditions. When President Grover Cleveland was in charge, the United States faced an economic depression. Five hundred banks perished, 15,000 companies went bankrupt, and many farms stopped producing crops. Though

Cleveland believed that the government should not carry out proactive economic policies, in 1894 he sent in federal troops when a railroad strike prevented the delivery of the mail. People believed that Cleveland was responsible for the economic depression. Even though Cleveland was a Democrat, he favored strong government like a Republican. But as for financial strategy, he believed it best to give more power to the private sector.

As we have mentioned, from the beginning of the United States, people and politicians have been divided into two opinions. Some people say they need a strong federal government, and others insist they need to maintain local power more than central government. This was one of the causes of the Civil War. And even after the era of Reconstruction, U.S. politics had been divided over this subject in economic policy, as we have seen in the case of President Cleveland.

By the beginning of the 20th century the West was fully developed. There was no more frontier in the U.S. America became interested in further expansion into the Pacific and the Caribbean Sea.

In 1898 the United States went to war against Spain over the control of Cuba. America had an economic interest in Cuba, while Cuba itself was fighting against Spanish rule. The Spanish–American War began and ended in the same year. The "Rough Riders," America's first volunteer soldiers led by Theodore Roosevelt, played a significant role in the Cuban fighting. After a treaty was signed in December, Spain gave up control of Cuba, Puerto Rico, and Guam to the United States. In 1902 Cuba became an independent nation.

In the course of the war the Philippines also came under American control after U.S. battleships defeated the Spanish off the coast of Manila. Filipino revolutionists under the leadership of Emilio Aguinaldo supported the United States in the war, but after the war America opposed the independence of the Philippines. Aguinaldo decided to fight against America. However, the Philippine–American War ended in 1902 in his defeat. This was during the time of President William McKinley.

McKinley was re-elected president in 1900 but was killed a year later by the anarchist Leon Czolgosz at the Pan-American

Theodore Roosevelt

Exposition. Vice President Theodore Roosevelt succeeded McKinley in office.

Construction of the Panama Canal began in 1903. After a diplomatic battle with Columbia, which controlled Panama at that time, the U.S. acquired possession of the canal when it was opened in 1914. The site was called the Canal Zone, and it remained under American control until the end of 1999.

Chapter 6

World War I and American Prosperity

第6章

成長を続けるアメリカには、経済的な夢と自由を求め、世界中から移民が押し寄せます。そして、彼らのもたらした労働力と知恵、そしてそこから生まれる産業と富によって、アメリカは世界の強国へと変貌を遂げるのです。その頃、ヨーロッパでは列強が植民地やヨーロッパでの利権をめぐって混乱が続いていました。その混乱が第一次世界大戦へと発展し、やがてアメリカも参戦します。戦争が終わったとき、ヨーロッパは疲弊し、アメリカは世界最大の債権国となったのです。戦後のアメリカの繁栄は、斬新なアメリカの都市文化が世界に輸出されはじめた時代でもありました。しかし、アメリカの経済が大恐慌によって破綻した時、世界は再び次の戦争へと突き進んでいったのでした。

第6章で使われている用語です。わからない語は巻末のワードリストで確認しましょう。

- [ ] aftermath
- [ ] compensation
- [ ] contradiction
- [ ] devastate
- [ ] dictator
- [ ] dominant
- [ ] navigation
- [ ] outlawing
- [ ] reduction
- [ ] take up
- [ ] turbulence
- [ ] unethical

THE PERIOD BEFORE THE FIRST WORLD WAR

In 1904 Theodore Roosevelt was elected for his second term as president. He dealt with issues of corruption in the business sector and faced a financial crisis during the Panic of 1907. Even though the U.S. faced such challenges, it gradually became the dominant power in the world. Why was this? It occurred because of the migration of people from all over the world. In the first and second decades of the 20th century, due to the wars and political turbulence in Europe, countless immigrants crossed the Atlantic Ocean. America became the land of opportunity, freedom, and safety for these people. America became a vast pool of consumers as well as laborers.

More importantly, America contained the intense energy of people who were seeking to survive and succeed. Of course, the reality was not easy. Big business caused labor issues; the gap between rich and poor was widening; and labor strikes spread throughout the country from 1910 to 1920. Despite such social contradictions, the steel, oil, automobile, and public utility industries became significant sectors that would influence business culture in the U.S. for years to come.

In 1886 Richard Warren Sears started a mail order business in Chicago. He sent catalogues to immigrants and pioneers spread all over the United States to sell the commodities they needed. His business was one of the typical venture businesses at that time when the United States was expanding its population and territories.

In 1903 the Wright brothers invented the first successful airplane. In 1908 Ford Motor Company started to sell the Ford Model T as the first affordable automobile for the ordinary citizen. The U.S. economy and business began to lead the world.

In 1912 the Democrat Woodrow Wilson was elected president. During his term, in 1913, the Federal Reserve System was created, which gave control of the monetary system to the federal government. The Clayton Anti-Trust Act of 1914 and the Federal Trade Commission, established the same year, provided additional protection for consumers.

THE FIRST WORLD WAR AND ITS AFTERMATH

While the U.S. was developing as a nation, Europe was facing many problems. Major countries confronted each other for control over the world.

Chapter 6 World War I and American Prosperity

When the Ottoman Empire declined, many regions formerly under its control attempted to become independent. Britain, France, Russia, Germany, and Austria wanted to influence them.

Finally, after a series of battles, World War I broke out in 1914. At first President Wilson tried to remain neutral. However, after German submarines sank American merchant ships, the U.S. became involved. War was declared on Germany in April 1917.

To prepare for the war, the United States trained more than four million soldiers. It was the most significant number of troops the U.S. would ever send to war. In nineteen months more than two million of these soldiers were sent to fight abroad. This was the moment when America became actively involved in world affairs following the declaration of the Monroe Doctrine. The war itself was terribly cruel. A total of 126,000 American soldiers were killed, and 234,000 were wounded.

World War I ended in November 1918. Europe was devastated. The U.S.

Poster recruiting soldiers for World War I

had become the largest creditor nation in the world.

President Wilson proposed Fourteen Points in January 1918 to create a new order for the postwar period. It included the reduction of armaments, freedom of navigation, and the creation of an international association to keep the peace. Based on these ideas, the League of Nations was established.

However, the major countries among the Allies ignored most of the Fourteen Points when drafting the Treaty of Versailles, which would bring the war to an end. They also demanded that Germany pay them a large sum of money in compensation for wartime losses. Above all, the United States never joined the League since Congress refused involvement.

The 1920s were an era of postwar success. By 1930 the population in the United States had

Jazz gained nationwide popularity in the 1920s and 1930s

grown to 122.77 million. This era was called the Jazz Age. American culture began to grow in unique directions. In cities like New York there were many creative artists. They introduced jazz music, Broadway musicals, and many experimental literary works. City culture also influenced social movements. Protesting discrimination against black people and promoting socialism became popular. In 1920 the Nineteenth Amendment gave women the right to vote.

In the early 20th century, commercial airplanes were a significant development in the transportation of goods, and in the 1920s they began to carry passengers and mail as well. Also, Charles A. Lindbergh became the first person to fly across the Atlantic. Shortly after that, in 1933, Wiley Post completed the first solo flight around the world.

On the other hand, some people could not accept such new movements. The majority of Americans were strict Protestants. First of all,

Charles Lindbergh with the Spirit of St. Louis

Removal of liquor during Prohibition (1920-1933)

they considered the drinking of alcohol to be unethical. In 1920 Congress put Prohibition into effect, that is, the outlawing of the making an drinking of alcohol, which lasted until 1933. In the countryside, above all in the South, some people took up the idea of radical racism. They organized the Ku Klux Klan to suppress blacks. Discrimination was carried out not only against blacks but also against many new immigrants, such as those from Asia.

During the term of President Calvin Coolidge, Congress decided to restrict immigration. In 1910, out of the 92 million people living in the United States, 12 million had been born overseas. In 1924 the government limited the number of immigrants from Eastern Europe and Asia.

Chapter 6 World War I and American Prosperity

DEPRESSION AND THE PATH TOWARD THE SECOND WORLD WAR

American prosperity after World War I was dependent on a so-called bubble economy based on overinvestment. Finally the bubble burst.

On October 24, 1929, the stock market crashed. It was one of the worst financial events in American history and ended the country's postwar prosperity. Unemployment and bank failures were huge. The period after the stock market crash is known as the Great Depression. The Depression spread around the world. At first, President Hoover thought that there was no need for him to act, and everything would be all right in the end. However, the situation did not improve.

In 1932 the Democrat Franklin D. Roosevelt was elected president. He ordered Congress to hold a

American Union Bank in New York during the Depression

special session to improve the economic situation, but the laws they made did not solve the problem.

So the federal government took the lead in the form of federal emergency measures, which included providing money to the National Recovery Admin-

Franklin D. Roosevelt served as the 32nd president of the United States

istration, Agricultural Adjustment Administration, and National Labor Relations Board to helped reduce some of the economic problems and provide jobs. Also, public building projects were started to create more jobs, and the banking system was improved. While the government created various programs to fix the economy, it had to spend a great deal of money on them and was criticized for that. These reforms and public works projects were named the "New Deal."

In 1936 the governor of Kansas, Alfred M. Landon, a Republican, ran for president against Franklin D. Roosevelt. Landon severely criticized Roosevelt's policies, but was defeated. Roosevelt won in all the states, except for two: Maine and Vermont.

Labor movements became stronger in the middle

Chapter 6 World War I and American Prosperity

of the 1930s, particularly in large industries such as steel and automobiles. In 1936 the Committee for Industrial Organization was founded to organize these unions.

Due to the frustration caused by the Great Depression, many people throughout the world wanted strong governments that could provide practical solutions. In Germany, Hitler's Nazi Party was elected to lead their country, and Hitler eventually became a dictator. The same thing happened in Italy under Mussolini. Germany was a significant threat to other European countries because the Nazis did not hesitate to invade neighbors where Germany had an interest.

In Asia, Japan rose and grew in military power. In 1931 it invaded China. This threatened America's economic interests in the Far East. In 1940 Germany, Italy, and Japan became allies. The U.S. needed to prepare for war again.

Chapter 7

America in the World

第7章

第二次世界大戦は、アメリカとイギリス、そしてソ連とが連携してドイツ、イタリア、そして日本を破った戦争でした。それは過去に類をみない残酷な殺戮の記憶を人々に残した戦争でもありました。戦後、アメリカとソ連とが対立し、冷戦の時代を迎えながらも、その記憶が両国の衝突を最終的に防いできたのです。しかし、超大国となったアメリカは、ソ連や中国に対抗し、しばしば世界各地の紛争に介入します。特にベトナム戦争では膨大な犠牲をはらうことになりました。その過程で、アメリカ国内でも新たな人権をめぐる大衆運動が繰り広げられ、全ての人に平等な権利が認められた公民権法も成立しました。成熟したアメリカが、ソ連の崩壊と共により多様で複雑になった世界とどう対応してゆくのか。アメリカを見舞った同時多発テロ事件の後、そしてIT革命やリーマンショックが世界を見舞った後、これからのアメリカがどう世界とかかわってゆくのか。アメリカ社会はこうした環境の変化を受けながら、未来への期待と不安の中で揺れ動いているのです。

第7章で使われている用語です。わからない語は巻末のワードリストで確認しましょう。

- [ ] advocate
- [ ] détente
- [ ] denounce
- [ ] distrust
- [ ] diversity
- [ ] drug cartel
- [ ] fraud
- [ ] outrage
- [ ] prejudice
- [ ] restore
- [ ] tactics
- [ ] unconditional

ENTERING INTO THE SECOND WORLD WAR

When the war began in Europe in 1939, the United States quickly declared that it would be neutral. However, Congress decided to lend and sell weapons to Allies in Europe. At the same time, America increased its military strength to a very high level.

Because of the war time emergency, an exception was made to the unofficial rule that a president could run for only two terms. Roosevelt was re-elected for a third term after defeating Wendell L. Willkie.

Around that time, the U.S. and Japan were negotiating to seek peace. However, in December 1941 Imperial Japanese Navy airplanes suddenly attacked Pearl Harbor, a naval base in Hawaii. So the United States entered World War II, and Germany and Italy declared war on the U.S. a short while later. At the beginning of the war, Japanese forces captured the Philippines and took control of Southeast Asia.

In 1943 the U.S. Navy started fighting back. Japan withdrew from Guadalcanal in the Solomon Islands, and the United States won back land it had lost before the war. Under the leadership of Admirals Nimitz and Halsey, the U.S. Navy defeated the

Japanese Navy at Midway and in a series of battles in the southern Pacific area. By March 1945 the Philippines belonged to the U.S. again. Also in 1945 the U.S. Navy invaded Iwo-Jima and Okinawa.

On the European front, Russia retreated when Germany invaded. Germany took control of France and many other European nations. However, it was gradually pushed back from Russian territory.

Cooperation between countries was crucial during the war. There was a close relationship between the leaders of the "Big Three" (the United States, Great Britain, and the Soviet Union). Especially close was the relationship between the United States and Great Britain, which was established by the Atlantic Conference in 1941. The Conference produced the Atlantic Charter, a postwar plan for the world. The Charter wanted worldwide peace, freedom, and

USS West Virginia, sunk during the Japanese attack on Pearl Harbor

Chapter 7 America in the World

security, and suggested creating a new international organization to maintain peace.

Based on this agreement, Roosevelt created the name "United Nations" to describe the Allies. It was later used as the name of the international organization that exists today.

After the Moscow Conference of Foreign Ministers, which was held in October 1943, there were successful international conferences in Cairo, Egypt, and Iran. During the Cairo Conference in November, the Allies made some decisions about Japan and plans for a postwar Asia.

The next summer, in 1944, an international conference was held in New Hampshire in the U.S. to create an international bank to help the world improve financially. At the Yalta Conferences in February 1945, the Allies came up with a system

Big Three at the Yalta Conference

to keep world peace as well as final plans to defeat Germany. However, two months after the Yalta Conference, President Roosevelt suddenly died, and Harry S. Truman became the next president. President Roosevelt was the only president to serve four terms in U.S. history.

TOWARD THE END OF WORLD WAR II
Earlier, in August 1943, Italy had surrendered, so the Allies had hoped that World War II would end in 1944.

On June 6, 1944, President Roosevelt had announced the invasion of Normandy in France, and by August the Allies had freed Paris and were marching on Germany. Finally, when Russian troops came into Berlin in April 1945, Adolf Hitler killed himself. Germany then agreed to unconditional surrender after nearly six, long years of the most intense fighting the world had ever seen.

Millions of American men had joined the military, and the number reached 13 million by 1944. Many women did the jobs that men normally did in various industries. Other women joined the army to undertake work such as nursing, and some joined the Women's Army Corps.

In the Pacific, both the U.S. and Japan lost many

Chapter 7 America in the World

lives. The United States was further concerned about the postwar influence of the Soviet Union in Japan, and therefore wanted to end the war as soon as possible. It decided to use nuclear weapons. On August 6, 1945, an atomic bomb was dropped on the Japanese city of Hiroshima, and another one on Nagasaki on August 9. Due to the heat wave, countless people, including civilians, died instantly. More than 200,000 people died within a few months in both cities. It is still a matter of debate whether it was right to use such a destructive weapon. However, it is true that this was a factor in Japan's decision to surrender. Soon after, Russia declared war against Japan and invaded Manchuria. The war in the Pacific ended shortly after that.

The Japanese government agreed to surrender according to the terms of the Potsdam Declaration issued in July 26, 1945. After a series of negotiations, the official announcement of the surrender was made on August 14,

Mushroom cloud from the atomic explosion in Nagasaki

1945; this marked the end of World War II.

Japan accepted General Douglas MacArthur as Supreme Commander of the Allied Powers in Japan, and the Japanese emperor was allowed to remain as the nation's symbolic leader.

MacArthur smoking pipe in Manila

World War II saw approximately 410,000 American lives lost. More than 60,000,000 people, including civilians, were killed in both Allied nations and Axis nations. In Europe Nazi Germany massacred more than 5 million Jews. World War II was the most tragic war in human history.

PEACE AND THE WAR'S AFTERMATH

Despite the death of President Roosevelt, a conference to establish the United Nations took place as planned on April 25, 1945. The United Nations Charter for a World Security Organization was made by representatives of 50 nations during eight weeks of discussion. The Charter set up six main organizations: the General Assembly, the Security Council, the Economic and Social Council, the Trusteeship

Chapter 7 America in the World

Council, the International Court of Justice, and the Secretariat. The United States was the first nation to join the organization.

After the war America experienced some problems with economic recovery, employment, and soldiers coming home and trying to get used to everyday life again. The United States also had to help Europe and Japan recover from the war and to avoid the increase of Soviet influence.

In fact, the United States and the Soviet Union became the most powerful nations in the world. The Soviet Union controlled the countries it had entered during the war and established Communist governments in those countries. In the meantime, the United States, along with its allies Great Britain and France, maintained military forces in West Germany. The primary topic of U.S. foreign policy was how to stop Soviet expansion.

In the years after the end of the war President Truman faced various social and financial problems as the American people wanted to have high living standards again. At the same time, the Republican Party didn't like the New Deal programs and didn't want to be involved in helping other countries make an economic recovery.

In answer to this, President Truman established

a "Fair Deal" program to improve living standards and wages. The program included measures to strengthen social security, housing policies, and working conditions.

A series of strikes that began in 1945 led to the Labor Management Relations Act of 1947, also known as the Taft–Hartley Act, which aimed to protect workers from unfair labor practices and to limit the power of large companies. As a result, wages were increased and working hours were reduced. During this time the economy began to pick up. Production levels rose, and wages and prices increased. In 1948 Truman was elected president.

On the other hand, tensions between the United States and the Communist nations led by the Soviet Union had reached a point where Cold War policies were a part of everyday life. Soviet troops

People in Berlin watching United States Air Force planes

CHAPTER 7 AMERICA IN THE WORLD

had occupied East Berlin in 1948. West Berlin was under the control of the United States, the United Kingdom, and France, leading the Soviet Union to block all railroads and roads between Berlin and Western countries. The "Berlin Airlift" succeeded in getting food and basic necessities to West Berlin. After this incident, Germany gave up forming a single country. West Germany became the Federal Republic of Germany, and East Germany became the German Democratic Republic.

AMERICA AS THE SUPERPOWER

"Cold war" was the term used to describe the tension between the United States and its allies and the countries under the influence of the Soviet Union. The wars were not always "cold," however; some of them were hot.

United States Army near the Kum River during the Korean War

Along with the end of World War II, Korea became independent from Japan. However, the nation was divided between North and South. The major conflict of the Cold War began in June 1950 when Communist North Korea invaded democratic South Korea. To stop Communism from spreading across all of the Korean Peninsula, President Truman sent U.S. military forces to help South Korea. But neither the U.S. nor North Korea could win a complete victory. Eventually they stopped fighting in July 1953. The 38th parallel marks the boundary between North and South Korea. In China the Communist party united the country in 1949. China helped North Korea in the fighting against the U.S.

As the most powerful and wealthy nation in the world, the United States had a role to play as the leader of international society. In 1952 the United States, together with former Allied countries except for the Soviet Union, signed a peace treaty with Japan. Furthermore, the U.S. signed a security treaty with Japan to protect its interests in the Far East. In the same year the Republican Dwight D. Eisenhower became president, and he decided to give economic aid to European nations.

In the 1950s the American lifestyle was evolving. Television sets spread to many homes throughout

Chapter 7 America in the World

In the 1950s, Americans enjoyed economic growth and prosperity; Ford Thunderbird, 1958; Popular singer Elvis Presley

the country. The electronics, frozen foods, and plastics industries introduced many new products. The population grew by 28 million within ten years, and the increased population led to an increase in the demand for consumer goods.

Along with these changes, civil rights issues were now receiving attention. In 1954 the Supreme Court decided that all students, black and white, should be able to study at all public schools in the country. Civil rights leaders continued to seek equality in every part of life, but this was not welcomed by many people. In 1957 President Eisenhower had to send troops to protect black students going to school in Little Rock, Arkansas.

Eisenhower's "Modern Republicanism" policy focused on creating better federal government systems and reducing spending. But when the first man-made satellites (Sputnik I and Sputnik II) were launched by the Soviet Union in November 1957, he quickly demanded improvements in the space technology program and federal assistance for schools to improve science education. Beyond a doubt, the Soviet Union's achievements in space showed that America had fallen behind in space technology. The influence of Communism was quite visible around the end of the second term of President Eisenhower. The Viet Cong attacked the U.S.-supported government in South Vietnam. Also, the Communist leader Fidel Castro came to power in Cuba in 1959. Eisenhower cut diplomatic ties with Cuba in 1961.

KENNEDY AND THE CUBAN CRISIS

John F. Kennedy of the Democratic Party won the presidency in 1960 in one of the closest elections in U.S. history. During the election, debates between Kennedy and his opponent, Richard M. Nixon, a Republican, were shown on television throughout the country. Immediately after taking office, Kennedy began his "New Frontier" program, which was similar to Roosevelt's New Deal. In Congress he explained his plan to achieve economic growth, reform taxes, save natural resources, and encourage

Chapter 7 America in the World

housing and development in cities. In the speech he gave when he took office, he said that it was necessary to continue to fight against Communism.

John F. Kennedy at the White House

The relationship between Kennedy and the Soviet leader Nikita Khrushchev grew worse over the next year and a half. After learning that the Soviets were building nuclear missile bases in Cuba, Kennedy decided to block off the sea around Cuba. This could have led to total war between the two superpowers, but the Soviets decided to withdraw their missiles from the island. War was avoided.

In 1963 Kennedy succeeded in getting the Soviet Union to sign a Nuclear Test Ban Treaty. The Treaty placed limits on the testing of nuclear weapons in space, water, and the atmosphere. He also promoted efforts to put U.S. astronauts on the moon and restore America's leadership in space. Kennedy also sent American soldiers to Vietnam to fight the Viet Cong.

Unfortunately, Kennedy was assassinated in Dallas, Texas, on November 22, 1963. Vice President

Lyndon B. Johnson became the president and continued the New Frontier program.

Major policies during Johnson's presidency included the Tax Reform Act of 1964. Johnson was nominated as the Democratic presidential candidate in 1964, and due to the continued public support for the New Frontier program, he easily defeated Barry M. Goldwater, the Republican candidate.

Johnson carried out his vision of a "Great Society" and put in place what would later become national social programs such as Medicare to help the elderly and disabled. Johnson also tried to create a better school system through Head Start and to make progress on civil rights issues.

THE CHALLENGES AND TURBULENCE OF THE SIXTIES

The 1960s were an era of turbulence. It was a decade of anger and reconciliation. The storm of the Civil Rights movement for equality between white and black divided the nation.

Martin Luther King Jr. led the movement to abolish the Jim Crow laws. His philosophy of fighting without the use of violence gained many supporters throughout the country. However, discrimination in the Southern states was deep and widespread. Other

Chapter 7 America in the World

black activists, such as Malcolm X, advocated violent methods. Uprisings and riots by frustrated blacks occurred everywhere.

John F. Kennedy supported Martin Luther King Jr. in his efforts to establish the Civil Rights Act and treat people equally. The law passed Congress in 1964. It was a moment to be remembered in the struggle for equality and human rights.

Sadly, both Malcolm X and Martin Luther King Jr. fell victims to assassins. These incidents are black marks in American history.

While Americans struggled internally to create the Civil Rights Act, the U.S. government faced another issue—the war against Communism in Vietnam.

Many Americans thought that it was their duty to protect the democratic world, and supporting South Vietnam was good for the stability and safety of Southeastern Asia. However, from the Vietnamese

March on Washington for Jobs and Freedom, 1963

point of view, who had just become independent from French rule, the U.S. was just another invader.

In the tropical jungles and mountains of Vietnam, the Viet Cong resisted American troops with persistent guerrilla tactics. During the fighting many brutal scenes involving U.S. soldiers were reported by the mass media to the world. This gave rise to anger and outrage at the American government. Many people argued that the war should be brought to an end. This antiwar movement joined hands with the Civil Rights movement to become an even more powerful force. Thus American society faced severe challenges both domestically and internationally.

In 1968 President Johnson sent more than 500,000 soldiers to Vietnam, and the war escalated. Antiwar demonstrations spread across the nation. In March Johnson said that he would stop the U.S. bombing of North Vietnam and that he would not run for another presidential term. In the election of 1968, Republican candidate Richard Nixon became president.

Nixon entered office in 1969 and decided that U.S. troops should leave Vietnam. The United States remained divided about the Vietnam War. Some believed in the continuation of the war, but others wanted U.S. soldiers to return home. Peace talks

Chapter 7 America in the World

Viet Cong guerrilla in combat

were held in Paris in 1969, but they were unsuccessful. It took another four years before the U.S. army would leave Vietnam.

While Americans were puzzled and disappointed by the Vietnam War, they were encouraged by one achievement. In July 1969 Neil A. Armstrong and Edwin E. Aldrin Jr. became the first human beings to walk on the surface of the moon. America was once again ahead of the Soviet Union in the space race.

A DIVIDED SOCIETY AFTER VIETNAM

As a superpower America thought that it could export the American way of life to the rest of the world and that it would be accepted. They considered freedom, democracy, and a free economy to be exportable products.

However, every region and country in the world

has its own history and way of life. Through the Vietnam War Americans learned that they are not always accepted.

After the end of the Vietnam War, Nixon tried to improve America's relationship with Communist countries. This is called détente. Both America and the Soviet Union agreed to reduce the number of nuclear weapons. In the efforts to build ties with the Soviet Union and the People's Republic of China, Nixon visited both nations in 1972. During the summit meeting in the Soviet Union, a critical arms treaty was signed by Nixon and the Communist Party leader Leonid Brezhnev. In the same year Nixon won his second term as president. In early 1973 a peace treaty (The Paris Peace Accords) was signed, ending military action and bringing temporary peace between North and South Vietnam.

In the following year a political scandal hit the Nixon administration. The president was linked to a break-in at the Democratic National Committee Headquarters that had taken place in 1972. This event became known as the Watergate scandal. Also, Vice President Agnew resigned because he had illegally received money while serving in civil service positions in Maryland. The House Minority Leader, Gerald R. Ford, became vice president. The

Chapter 7 America in the World

Watergate scandal led to President Nixon's resignation on August 9, 1974. Gerald Ford became president.

Nixon's departure from the White House

Ford faced many challenges. Following the end of the Vietnam War, many returning soldiers had a hard time adjusting to life at home. The black community was still economically pressed, despite the passage of the Civil Rights Act. The distrust between the races remained heated. The distrust of the government grew even stronger when the president himself was involved in scandal.

Ford succeeded a little in restoring public trust in the political system, but there were still economic problems to deal with. He took on the challenge of inflation, but due to the oil crisis in 1973 and the cost of the Vietnam War, the nation fell into a recession. Major cities were devastated, and urban crime increased. In the presidential election of 1976, the Democrat James E. Carter defeated Ford.

In addition to inflation, President Carter also had to face energy issues. He urged large corporations to stop increasing prices and established a national energy program to reduce oil imports.

Carter's popularity dropped due to continued gasoline shortages and high inflation. He had some success, however, in foreign affairs. He sorted out the issue of whether the United States or Panama should control the Panama Canal. His efforts to improve foreign relations with the People's Republic of China resulted in an agreement between the two countries, which then led to diplomatic ties in 1979. The president was also involved in establishing a peace treaty between Israel and Egypt and in joint negotiations on SALT II (Strategic Arms Limitation Talks II).

However, Carter faced another challenge. When the Iranian Revolution occurred and the pro-U.S. government was abolished, Iranian activists occupied the U.S. embassy. Carter was unable to immediately solve this tension-filled situation.

THE END OF THE COLD WAR TO THE NEW GENERATION

In the presidential election of 1980 Carter was defeated by Ronald W. Reagan, the Republican candidate. Reagan wanted to create a revival of the American nation and society.

Chapter 7 America in the World

His goals included strengthening the political power of the states, building up the military, and lowering taxes and government spending. Congress mostly approved of his plans. Based on his policy of small federal government, the U.S. economy revived from the shock following the Vietnam War.

On the other hand, the situation in the Middle East became more and more complex. After Palestine lost its land inside Israel, Arab nations who supported Palestine fought several wars with Israel. Above all, after Saddam Hussein became the dictator of Iraq, the relationship between the two countries worsened.

After Reagan left office in 1989, George H. W. Bush, the vice president under Reagan, was elected president. During his term in office, President Bush faced war against Iraq, recessions, environmental issues, and educational reform. Above all, when Iraq occupied Kuwait in 1990, Bush decided to fight

Reagan and Gorbachev sign treaty at the White House, 1987

against Saddam Hussein. This is known as the Gulf War. In 1992 the United States and allied forces successfully removed Iraqi forces from Kuwait.

Drug issues were also highlighted during this period. The scandal involving the Bank of Credit and Commerce (BCCI) was, perhaps, one of the most complex problems in the banking system. The scandal involved five bank leaders secretly dealing with millions of dollars of Medellin drug cartel money. The executives were found guilty of fraud. Also around this time, Bush sent troops to Panama to capture General Manuel Noriega because of his involvement with drug money.

In the year 1991, after a chaotic series of economic and political events, the Soviet Union collapsed. Many countries under the Soviet Union's umbrella became independent and abandoned Communism. East Germany fell, and Germany was finally united as one nation. The Cold war came to an end.

This also marked the end of the postwar era following World War II. The European and Japanese economies had fully recovered, and they presented tough competition for American industries. More than that, the world became economically linked. Supported by computer technology, information began to be shared on a global scale.

Chapter 7 America in the World

Although the end of the Cold War meant the beginning of a new era, it has not been an easy path. The Middle East is still in chaos, and eastern Europe is the site of much conflict.

In the era of President Bill Clinton, the U.S. enjoyed an economic recovery. America led the world in innovation with the appearance of new businesses related to the Internet and IT solutions. Increased investment in these areas helped meet the innovative challenges of the day.

Around this time the government tightened the Civil Rights Act to reduce social tension. Many states created laws against discrimination. These laws applied not only to race, but also to religious background, sex, nationality, disability, and many other factors involving people's fundamental rights. There were significant improvements in human rights and respect for the diversity of people.

Germany reunited

FROM SEPTEMBER 11 TO THE PRESENT

In the morning of September 11, 2001, the world was shaken when an Islamic terrorist group attacked the U.S. The World Trade Center buildings, one of the symbols of New York City, and the Pentagon were destroyed by hijacked commercial airlines.

President George W. Bush, the son of George H. W. Bush, who was the newly elected Republican president, decided to attack Afghanistan, where the government supported terrorism.

The fighting spread, and eventually the U.S. invaded Iraq to remove the dictator Saddam Hussein. It was a controversial decision as Americans

The World Trade Center buildings after the attack by Islamic terrorists

Chapter 7 America in the World

still remembered the agony of the Vietnam War. Further, American involvement in Iraq created a wave of anger among Arabs. It was a chain reaction. Angry passion created new terrorism, and new terrorism created more passionate anger. This vicious cycle has yet to be solved today.

On the other hand, the birth of new technology created giant players who would lead the world from the U.S., such as Apple, Microsoft, Google, and Amazon. Many other American enterprises also played major roles in the new global Internet era. Most of these companies were founded by young entrepreneurs.

George W. Bush left office during a recession started by the bankruptcy of Lehman Brothers in 2008. Barack Obama became the 44th president of the United States. This was a historic moment since he was the first black president in American history. Since his background was different from other American leaders, liberals hoped for the development of a progressive society without prejudice, and they expected American culture to be a leader in respecting freedom and democracy. The relationship between the United States and Cuba improved after 50 years of tension. Obama also tried to reduce the American military presence in Afghanistan and

Iraq. Domestically he created a new health care system.

However, during his term the Middle East experienced another period of chaos as the terrorist group called the Islamic State became a worldwide threat known for its cruelty. Inside the United States, the gap between rich and poor could not be improved.

In January 2017 Obama's term was over. And everybody was surprised when Donald Trump, a New York real estate entrepreneur, was elected president. His supporters are conservative Americans who are opposed to having new immigrants, a global economy, and liberal solutions to ease the tension between races and different lifestyles. Trump's campaign slogan, "America First," represented these people's political view.

Epilogue

EPILOGUE TO THE UNKNOWN FUTURE

In these last twenty years technology has improved radically. From Internet solutions to Artificial Intelligence, from biotechnology to space technology, we are facing a neo-industrial revolution to the future. We need to learn how people can deal with these technologies for peace and prosperity.

We also face the question of how to protect the environment. Since human beings came into the possession of technology, more animals have become extinct than at any other time. America has played the major role in developing this technology over the last 100 years. Global warming is another serious challenge to our future.

In recent decades the division and gap between people has widened. Liberals and conservatives denounce each other as if they are sworn enemies. People don't know how to compromise to create a productive future.

As we saw in the era of the American Civil War, once people refuse to accept other people's ways of thinking, society itself will fall into ruin and savage conflict. Americans are now being asked to find a solution to this issue.

The American nation started out under the influence of Protestantism. Protestants asked for freedom of religion, and they valued hard work. The people who immigrated to the new world believed in the words of Benjamin Franklin, "Time is money." But they also believed in the concepts of freedom of the press, essential equality, and respect for the diversity of immigrant cultures. However, it has taken more than 400 years to achieve this goal since the first settlers arrival. And the process is not complete yet.

Without a doubt, immigrants added a special flavor to American society. Their frank and direct means of communication created a unique business culture. Sometimes they forget how unique they are, and when the United States became a global superpower, they tried to apply their ways to the rest of the world. However, we have yet to see if America is truly a global country.

As some neoconservatives insist, we need to know if the United States is nothing more than a Republic of immigrants. If answer is no, we have to invent a way of pursuing the traditional goals for the immigration society of the future. In other

Epilogue

words, we have to reconsider the meanings of the Declaration of Independence—"All men are created as equal"—in keeping with our century and times.

This is the question that Americans have before them—how to create their own future—and the answer to this question is still not known.

The 45th president of the United States, Donald Trump

Word List

- 本文で使われている全ての語を掲載しています(LEVEL 1、2)。ただし、LEVEL 3以上は、中学校レベルの語を含みません。
- 語形が規則変化する語の見出しは原形で示しています。不規則変化語は本文中で使われている形になっています。
- 一般的な意味を紹介していますので、一部の語で本文で実際に使われている品詞や意味と合っていないことがあります。
- 品詞は以下のように示しています。

名 名詞	代 代名詞	形 形容詞	副 副詞	動 動詞	助 助動詞
前 前置詞	接 接続詞	間 間投詞	冠 冠詞	略 略語	俗 俗語
頭 接頭語	尾 接尾語	別 記号	関 関係代名詞		

A

- **abandon** 動 捨てる, 放棄する
- **abolish** 動 廃止する, 撤廃する
- **abolitionist** 名 (法律・制度などの) 廃止論者
- **above all** 何よりも, 何にもまして
- **Abraham Lincoln** エイブラハム・リンカーン《第16代アメリカ合衆国大統領(任期1861-1865)》
- **accept** 動 ①受け入れる ②同意する, 認める
- **accord** 名 調和, 一致
- **according** 副 《-to ~》~によれば[よると]
- **achieve** 動 成し遂げる, 達成する, 成功を収める
- **achievement** 名 ①達成, 成就 ②業績
- **acquire** 動 獲得する, 確保する
- **act** 名 法令
- **active** 形 ①活動的な ②積極的な ③活動[作動]中の
- **actively** 副 活発に, 活動的に
- **activist** 名 活動家, 実践主義者
- **actually** 副 実際に, 本当に, 実は
- **add** 動 ①加える, 足す ②足し算をする ③言い添える
- **addition** 名 ①付加, 追加, 添加 ②足し算 in addition 加えて, さらに
- **additional** 形 追加の, さらなる
- **adjust** 動 ①適応する[させる], 慣れる ②調整する
- **adjustment** 名 ①調整, 調節 ②適応 ③調停
- **administration** 名 管理, 統治, 政権
- **admiral** 名 海軍提督, 艦隊司令官
- **admission** 名 ①入場(許可), 入会, 入学, 入社 ②入場料
- **admit** 動 認める, 許可する, 入れる be admitted to ~へ入るのを許される
- **Adolf Hitler** アドルフ・ヒトラー《ドイツの政治家。ドイツ国首相, および国家元首, 国家社会主義ドイツ労働者党(ナチス)の指導者(1889-1945)》
- **advanced** 形 上級の, 先に進んだ, 高等の
- **advancement** 名 進歩, 前進, 昇進
- **advantage** 名 有利な点[立場], 強み, 優越 take advantage of ~を利用する, ~につけ込む

Word List

- **advertisement** 名広告, 宣伝
- **advocate** 動主張する, 提唱する
- **affair** 名①事柄, 事件 ②《-s》業務, 仕事, やるべきこと **foreign affairs** 外務 **world affairs** 世界情勢
- **affect** 動影響する
- **affordable** 形手ごろな[良心的な]価格の
- **Afghanistan** 名アフガニスタン《国》
- **afraid of** 《be-》～を恐れる, ～を怖がる
- **Africa** 名アフリカ《大陸》
- **African** 形アフリカ(人)の 名アフリカ人
- **after** 熟 **after that** その後 **name after** ～にちなんで名付ける
- **aftermath** 名(事件などの)余波, 影響
- **afterward** 副その後, のちに
- **against** 熟 **stand up against** ～に抵抗する
- **age of** ～の時代
- **Agnew** 名スピロ・アグニュー《第39代アメリカ合衆国副大統領(1969-1973)》
- **agony** 名苦悩, 激しい苦痛
- **agreement** 名①合意, 協定 ②一致
- **agricultural** 形農業の, 農事の
- **agricultural Adjustment Administration** 農業調整局
- **agriculture** 名農業, 農耕
- **ahead of** ～より先[前]に, ～に先んじて
- **aid** 名援助(者), 助け **economic aid** 経済援助 **foreign aid** 対外援助
- **aim** 動ねらう, 目指す
- **air force** 空軍
- **airlift** 名(緊急の)空輸(体制)
- **airline** 名航空会社
- **airplane** 名飛行機
- **Alabama** 名アラバマ(州)
- **Alamo, battle of the** アラモの戦い《1836年2月23日～3月6日にメキシコ共和国軍とテキサス分離独立派の間で行われた戦闘》
- **Alaska** 名アラスカ(州)
- **alcohol** 名アルコール
- **Alexander Graham Bell** アレクサンダー・グラハム・ベル《スコットランド生まれの科学者, 発明家(1847-1922)》
- **Alexander H. Stephens** アレクサンダー・スティーヴンズ《アメリカ連合国初代副大統領(1812-1883)》
- **Alexander Hamilton** アレクサンダー・ハミルトン《アメリカ合衆国初代財務長官(1755-1804)》
- **Alfred M. Landon** アルフレッド・ランドン《カンザス州知事, 1936年の共和党大統領候補(1887-1987)》
- **all** 熟 **above all** 何よりも, 何にもまして **all over** ～中で, 全体に亘って, ～の至る所で **all over the world** 世界中に **all right** 大丈夫で, よろしい, 申し分ない **first of all** まず第一に
- **allied** 形同盟[連合]した, 関連した
- **Allied Powers** 連合国
- **allow** 動①許す,《-…to～》…が～するのを可能にする ②与える
- **ally** 名同盟国, 味方
- **along with** ～と一緒に
- **also** 熟 **not only ～ but also …** ～だけでなく…もまた
- **although** 接～だけれども, ～にもかかわらず, たとえ～でも
- **always** 熟 **not always** 必ずしも～であるとは限らない
- **Amazon** 名アマゾン・ドット・コム《アメリカに本拠を構えるECサイト》
- **amendment** 名①改正, 修正 ②(憲法の)改正案
- **America** 名アメリカ《国名・大陸》

A SHORT HISTORY OF AMERICA

- **American** 形 アメリカ(人)の 名 アメリカ人
- **American Civil War** 南北戦争《アメリカ合衆国の北部諸州とアメリカ連合国を称した南部諸州との間で行われた内戦(1861–1865)》
- **American Indian** アメリカインディアン
- **American Revolution** アメリカ独立革命
- **American Revolutionary War** アメリカ独立戦争(1775–1783)
- **American Union Bank** アメリカンユニオン銀行《大恐慌によって閉鎖された、ニューヨークの小規模都市銀行の一つ(1917–1931)》
- **American War of Independence** アメリカ独立戦争(1775–1783)
- **Amerigo Vespucci** アメリゴ・ヴェスプッチ《アメリカ州を探検したイタリアの探検家。新世界がアジアの一部ではなく、未知の四つ目の大陸であると論証した(1454–1512)》
- **amount** 名 量、額
- **anarchist** 名 無政府主義者、アナーキスト
- **Andrew Carnegie** アンドリュー・カーネギー《スコットランド生まれのアメリカの実業家(1835–1919)》
- **Andrew Jackson** アンドリュー・ジャクソン《第7代アメリカ合衆国大統領(任期1829–1837)》
- **Andrew Johnson** アンドリュー・ジョンソン《アメリカ合衆国の第16代副大統領および第17代大統領(任期1865–1869)》
- **anger** 名 怒り 動 怒る、〜を怒らせる
- **Anglican Church** 英国国教会、アングリカン・チャーチ
- **angry at** 《be–》〜に腹を立てている
- **Anne Hutchinson** アン・ハッチンソン《ピューリタンの認定されていない聖職者、マサチューセッツ、ロードアイランドおよびニューネーデルラントにおける先駆的開拓者(1591–1643)》
- **annex** 動 (武力などの)併合する
- **annexation** 名 併合
- **announce** 動 (人に)知らせる、公表する
- **announcement** 名 発表、アナウンス、告示、声明
- **answer** 熟 in answer to 〜に応じて
- **anti-slavery** 名形 奴隷制度廃止運動(の)
- **anti-trust** 形 反トラストの、独占禁止の
- **Antietam, Battle of** アンティータムの戦い《南北戦争の中盤1862年9月17日、メリーランド方面作戦の一環としてメリーランド州シャープスバーグ近く、およびアンティータム・クリークで行われた戦闘》
- **antiwar** 形 反戦の、戦争反対の
- **apart** 副 ①ばらばらに、離れて ②別にして、それだけで
- **appear** 動 ①現れる、見えてくる ②(〜のように)見える、〜らしい
- **appearance** 名 ①現れること、出現 ②外見、印象
- **apply** 動 ①あてはまる ②適用する
- **appoint** 動 任命する、指名する
- **Appomattox Court House, Battle of** アポマトックス・コートハウスの戦い《南北戦争の最終盤1865年4月9日にアポマトックス方面作戦の最後としてバージニア州アポマトックス郡で行われた戦い》
- **approach** 動 接近、(〜へ)近づく道
- **approve** 動 賛成する、承認する
- **approximately** 副 おおよそ、だいたい
- **Arab** 名 アラビア人、アラブ民族、

WORD LIST

アラブ 形アラブ(人)の
- **archeological** 形考古学の[に関する・的な]
- **argue** 動①論じる, 議論する ②主張する
- **Arizona** 名アリゾナ州
- **Arkansas** 名アーカンソー州
- **Armada** 名(スペインの)無敵艦隊
- **armament** 名武器, 軍備
- **army** 名軍隊, 《the-》陸軍
- **arose** 動arise(起こる)の過去
- **arrest** 動逮捕する
- **arrival** 名①到着 ②到達
- **artificial** 形人工的な
- **Artificial Intelligence** 人工知能
- **artist** 名芸術家
- **as** 熟 as a result その結果(として) as a result of ~の結果(として) as ~ as possible できるだけ~ as for ~に関しては, ~はどうかと言うと as if あたかも~のように, まるで~みたいに as soon as ~するとすぐ, ~するや否や as well なお, その上, 同様に as well as ~と同様に at the same time as ~と同時に be known as ~として知られている be seen as ~として見られる just as (ちょうど)であろうとおり see ~ as … ~を…と考える such as たとえば~, ~のような
- **Asia** 名アジア
- **assassin** 名暗殺者
- **assassinate** 動暗殺する
- **assembly** 名下院, 議会
- **assertive** 形断定的な, 独断的な
- **assistance** 名援助, 支援
- **association** 名①交際, 連合, 結合 ②協会, 組合
- **astronaut** 名宇宙飛行士
- **Atlantic** 形大西洋の 名《the-》大西洋
- **Atlantic Ocean** 大西洋
- **atmosphere** 名①大気, 空気 ②雰囲気
- **atomic** 形原子[原子力・原子力爆弾]の[に関する]
- **attack** 動襲う, 攻める
- **attacker** 名①撃者, 敵
- **attempt** 動試みる, 企てる
- **attention** 名注意, 集中
- **Austria** 名オーストリア《国名》
- **author** 名著者, 作家
- **automobile** 名自動車
- **autonomy** 名自治(権), 自律(性), 自主(性)
- **avoid** 動避ける, (~を)しないようにする
- **Axis** 名枢軸国
- **Aztec empire** アステカ王国

B

- **background** 名背景, 前歴, 生い立ち
- **Baltimore** 名ボルチモア(メリーランド州)《都市名》
- **Baltimore and Ohio Railroad** ボルチモア・アンド・オハイオ鉄道《アメリカ最古の鉄道のひとつ。1826年開通》
- **ban** 名禁止, 禁制
- **Bank of Credit and Commerce International** 国際商業信用銀行《かつてルクセンブルクを本拠に発展途上国を中心に営業していた銀行。略称BCCI》
- **banker** 名銀行家[員]
- **banking** 名銀行業務
- **bankrupt** 名破産(者)
- **bankruptcy** 名破産, 倒産
- **Barack Obama** バラク・オバマ

A Short History of America

《第44代アメリカ合衆国大統領(任期 2009–2017)》

- **Barry M. Goldwater** バリー・ゴールドウォーター《アメリカ合衆国の政治家。1964年の共和党大統領候補(1909–1998)》
- **base** 名 基地 動《– on ～》～に基礎を置く,基づく be based on ～に基づく
- **basic** 形 基礎の,基本の
- **battle** 名 戦闘,戦い
- **Battle of Antietam** アンティータムの戦い《南北戦争の中盤1862年9月17日,メリーランド方面作戦の一環としてメリーランド州シャープスバーグ近く,およびアンティータム・クリークで行われた戦闘》
- **Battle of Appomattox Court House** アポマトックス・コートハウスの戦い《南北戦争の最終盤1865年4月9日にアポマトックス方面作戦の最後としてバージニア州アポマトックス郡で行われた戦い》
- **Battle of Chickamauga** チカマウガの戦い《南北戦争の西部戦線における,テネシー州中南部とジョージア州北西部で1863年9月18日から20日に行われた戦闘》
- **Battle of Fort Sumter** サムター要塞の戦い《1861年4月12日から4月14日にかけて行なわれた戦闘。南北戦争の発端とされる戦い》
- **Battle of Gettysburg** ゲティスバーグの戦い《南北戦争において事実上の決戦となった戦い(1863)》
- **Battle of Hampton Roads** ハンプトン・ローズ海戦《南北戦争中に生起した海戦。鉄板で装甲された動力軍艦同士の歴史上最初の戦い(1862)》
- **Battle of Lexington and Concord** レキシントン・コンコードの戦い《1775年4月19日に起こった,アメリカ独立戦争が始まる契機となった英米間の戦闘》
- **Battle of Long Island** ロングアイランドの戦い《1776年8月22日から同年8月30日にかけて,現在のニューヨーク市ブルックリンを主戦場にして戦われた,アメリカ独立戦争の主要な戦闘のひとつ》
- **battle of Quebec** ケベックの戦い《アメリカ独立戦争初期の大陸軍によるカナダ侵攻作戦中,1775年12月31日にケベック市を守るイギリス軍との間に行われた戦闘》
- **battle of Queenston Heights** クイーンストン・ハイツの戦い《米英戦争の初期である1812年10月13日に,現在のオンタリオ州クィーンストン近くでイギリス軍とアメリカ軍との間に戦われた戦闘》
- **battle of the Alamo** アラモの戦い《テキサス独立戦争中の1836年2月23日～3月6日の13日間にメキシコ共和国軍とテキサス分離独立派の間で行われた戦闘》
- **battleship** 名 戦艦
- **bay** 名 湾,入り江
- **BCCI** 国際商業信用銀行《かつてルクセンブルクを本拠に発展途上国を中心に営業していた銀行。Bank of Credit and Commerce Internationalの略称》
- **beaver** 名 ビーバー《動物》
- **because of** ～のために,～の理由で
- **beef** 名 牛肉
- **begin with** ～で始まる
- **beginning** 名 初め,始まり
- **behind** 副 ①後ろに,背後に ②遅れて,劣って fall behind 取り残される,後れを取る
- **being** 名 存在,生命,人間 human being 人,人間
- **belief** 名 信じること,信念,信用
- **believe in** ～を信じる
- **belong** 動《– to ～》～に属する,～のものである

WORD LIST

- **benefit** 名利益, 恩恵
- **Benjamin Franklin** ベンジャミン・フランクリン《アメリカ合衆国の政治家, 外交官, 著述家, 物理学者, 気象学者(1706-1705)》
- **Bering Strait** ベーリング海峡
- **Berlin** 名ベルリン《ドイツの首都》
- **Berlin Airlift** ベルリン大空輸《1948年東西冷戦の切っ掛けとなったベルリン封鎖から西ベルリン市民を救済するために, 米空軍が, 唯一残された空路を使って大量の物資を運んだ》
- **beyond** 前～を越えて, ～の向こうに
- **bill** 名法案
- **Bill Clinton** ビル・クリントン《第42代アメリカ合衆国大統領(任期1993-2001)》
- **Bill of Rights** 権利章典《アメリカ合衆国における, 憲法中の人権保障規定。アメリカ合衆国憲法第1条から修正第10条の市民の基本的人権に関する規定》
- **billion** 形10億の, ばく大な, 無数の 名10億
- **biotechnology** 名バイオテクノロジー, 生物工学
- **birth** 名①出産, 誕生 ②生まれ, 起源, (よい)家柄
- **blueprint** 名青写真, 見取り図, 詳細な計画
- **board** 名委員会 動乗り込む
- **bomb** 名爆弾 動爆発する
- **bombing** 名爆撃, 爆破
- **border** 名境界, へり, 国境
- **Boston** 名ボストン(マサチューセッツ州)《都市名》
- **Boston Massacre** ボストン虐殺事件《1770年3月5日にマサチューセッツ湾直轄植民地のボストンでイギリス軍が民間人5人を虐殺した事件》
- **Boston Tea Party** ボストン茶会事件《1773年12月16日に, ボストンで, イギリス本国議会の植民地政策に憤慨した植民地人の急進派が港に停泊中の貨物輸送船に侵入し, イギリス東インド会社の船荷である紅茶箱を海に投棄した事件》
- **Bostonian** 名ボストン市民の愛称
- **both A and B** AもBも
- **boundary** 名境界線, 限界
- **bravely** 副勇敢に(も)
- **break out** 発生する, 急に起こる, (戦争が)勃発する
- **break up** ばらばらになる, 解散させる
- **break-in** 名不法侵入
- **breeze** 名そよ風
- **bring to an end** 終わらせる, ピリオドを打つ
- **Britain** 名大ブリテン(島)
- **British** 形①英国人の ②イギリス英語の 名英国人
- **British Parliament** イギリス議会
- **broad-minded** 形寛大な, 寛容な
- **Broadway musical** ブロードウェイ・ミュージカル
- **brutal** 形けもののような, 残酷な
- **bubble** 名泡, (泡のように実体のない)幻想
- **Buena Vista** ブエナ・ビスタ《メキシコ北部にある村》
- **buffalo** 名野牛, バッファロー
- **building** 名建物, 建造物, ビルディング
- **bulb** 名①電球 ②バルブ ③球根 light bulb 電球
- **Bull Run** 第一次ブルランの戦い《1861年7月21日にバージニア州マナサスの近くで行われた, 南北戦争の陸上戦闘では最初の大会戦》
- **Bunker Hill** バンカーヒルの戦い

A Short History of America

《アメリカ独立戦争初期, ボストン包囲戦中の1775年6月17日に起こった大陸軍とイギリス軍の戦闘》

- **bureau** 名 ①案内所, 事務所 ②局, 部
- **Burgesses, Virginia House of** バージニア植民地法府下院 《1619年にジェームズタウンで最初の議会が開催されたアメリカで最初の議会》
- **burst** 動 ①爆発する[させる] ②破裂する[させる]
- **businesspeople** 名 実業家, 経営者
- **by this time** この時までに, もうすでに

C

- **c.** 略 およそ, 約, ~年頃《= circa〈ラテン語〉》
- **cabin** 名 (丸太作りの)小屋, 船室, キャビン
- **cable** 名 ケーブル, 太綱
- **Cairo** 名 カイロ《エジプトの首都》
- **Cairo Conference** カイロ会議 《1943年11月23~27日, 連合国の首脳が, アジアでの戦略方針および対日処理方針を主要な議題として, エジプトのカイロで開催された会議》
- **California** 名 カリフォルニア《米国の州》
- **call for** ~を求める, 訴える, ~を呼び求める, 呼び出す
- **calm** 動 静まる, 静める
- **Calvin Coolidge** カルビン・クーリッジ《第30代アメリカ合衆国大統領(任期1923–1929)》
- **camera** 名 カメラ
- **campaign** 名 ①キャンペーン(活動, 運動) ②政治運動, 選挙運動
- **Canada** 名 カナダ《国名》
- **canal** 名 運河
- **Canal Zone** パナマ運河地帯《パナマ運河を取り囲んだアメリカ合衆国のかつての租借地, 海外領土》
- **cancel** 動 取り消す, 中止する
- **candidate** 名 立候補者
- **capital** 名 首都
- **captain** 名 長, 船長, 首領, 主将
- **capture** 動 捕える
- **care** health care 健康保険制度
- **Caribbean Sea** カリブ海
- **Carolina** 名 カロライナ植民地
- **carry out** 外へ運び出す, [計画を]実行する
- **cartel** 名 企業連合, カルテル drug cartel 麻薬カルテル《麻薬の製造・売買に関する活動を行う組織》
- **case** 熟 in the case of ~の場合は
- **Casimir Pulaski** カジミエシュ・プワスキ《ポーランド・リトアニア共和国の貴族, 軍人, 政治家。アメリカ独立戦争中の功績でアメリカ騎兵の父と呼ばれている(1746–1779)》
- **catalogue** 名 (商品の)目録, カタログ
- **Catholic** 形 カトリックの 名 カトリック教徒
- **celebrate** 動 ①祝う, 祝福する ②祝典を開く
- **central** 形 中央の, 主要な
- **centralized** 形 中央集権化の
- **certain** 形 ある
- **chain reaction** 連鎖反応
- **challenge** 名 ①挑戦 ②難関 動 挑む, 試す
- **chaos** 名 無秩序, 混乱状態
- **chaotic** 形 大混乱の, 雑然とした, 混沌とした
- **charge** 名 責任 in charge 責任を負って, 責任者で
- **Charles A. Lindbergh** チャールズ・リンドバーグ《アメリカ合

衆国の飛行家。1927年に大西洋単独無着陸飛行に初めて成功。1931年には北太平洋横断飛行にも成功した(1902-1974)》

- **Charles Mason** チャールズ・メイソン《イギリスの天文学者。1763年から1767年にわたって、ジェレマイア・ディクソンとともに、ペンシルベニア植民地とメリーランド植民地との境界線を確定したメイソン＝ディクソン線の測量をおこなった(1728-1786)》
- **Charter** 名 憲章
- **Chicago** 名 シカゴ(イリノイ州)《都市名》
- **Chickamauga, Battle of** チカマウガの戦い《南北戦争の西部戦線における、テネシー州中南部とジョージア州北西部で1863年9月18日から20日に行われた戦闘》
- **China** 名 中国《国名》
- **Chinese** 形 中国(人)の
- **choice** 名 選択
- **Christopher Columbus** クリストファー・コロンブス《探検家、航海者。大航海時代において、最初にアメリカ海域へ到達したイタリア人(1451-1506)》
- **citizen** 名 ①市民、国民 ②住民、民間人
- **citizenship** 名 公民権、市民権
- **civil** 形 ①一般人の、民間(人)の ②国内の、国家の ③礼儀正しい **civil service** (軍・司法・立法関係以外)政府官庁、(軍関係以外の)文官、公務員 **civil war** 内戦、内乱
- **Civil Rights Act** 1964年公民権法《アメリカ合衆国において人種差別を禁ずる法律。1950年代以降にアメリカ国内で活発化した、公民権運動を背景として1964年に合衆国連邦議会で成立した》
- **Civil Rights Bill** 公民権法案
- **Civil Rights movement** 公民権運動《1950年代なかばから1960年代なかばに、アフリカ系アメリカ人によりアメリカで展開された、差別の撤廃と法の下の平等、市民としての自由と権利を求める社会運動》
- **Civil War** 《The –》南北戦争《アメリカ合衆国の北部諸州とアメリカ連合国を称した南部諸州との間で行われた内戦(1961-1865)》
- **civilian** 名 一般市民、民間人
- **claim** 動 主張する
- **Clayton Anti-Trust Act** クレイトン法《1914年に制定された米国の連邦法で、反トラスト法の中心的な法律のひとつ》
- **clear** 形 はっきりした、明白な
- **closing** 名 終わり、閉鎖
- **co-educational** 形 男女共学の
- **coal** 名 石炭
- **coast** 名 海岸、沿岸
- **Coinage Act** 貨幣法《銀貨は補助貨幣となり、金銀複本位制が破棄され金本位制となった(1873)》
- **Cold War** 冷戦《第二次世界大戦後のアメリカを盟主とする資本主義・自由主義陣営と、ソ連を盟主とする共産主義・社会主義陣営との対立構造》
- **collapse** 動 崩壊する、崩れる、失敗する
- **colonial** 形 植民地の
- **colonial period** 植民地時代
- **colonist** 名 入植者
- **colonization** 名 植民地化
- **colonize** 動 植民する、入植する
- **colony** 名 植民[移民](地)
- **Colorado** 名 コロラド州
- **Columbia** 名 コロンビア共和国
- **columnist** 名 コラムニスト、特設欄執筆者
- **combat** 名 戦闘
- **come into** ～に入ってくる、～の状態になる

A Short History of America

- **come into conflict** 衝突[対立]する
- **come into operation** 動き始める, 作動し始める
- **come true** 実現する
- **come up with** 〜を思いつく, 考え出す, 見つけ出す
- **commander** 司令官, 指揮官
- **Commander-in-Chief** 名 最高司令官
- **Commanding General** 総司令官
- **commerce** 名 商業, 貿易
- **commercial** 形 商業の, 営利的な
- **commission** 名 (委任された職務を行う)委員会
- **committee** 名 評議会, 委員(会), 受託人
- **Committee for Industrial Organization** アメリカ労働総同盟・産業別組合会議
- **Common Sense** 『コモン・センス』《1776年1月よりトマス・ペインによって発行されたパンフレット。平易な英文でアメリカ合衆国の独立の必要性を説き, 合衆国独立への世論を強めさせた》
- **commonwealth** 名 民主国家, 共和国 Polish-Lithuanian Commonwealth ポーランド・リトアニア共和国(1569–1795)
- **communication** 名 伝えること, 伝導, 連絡
- **communism** 名 共産主義, 共産主義体制
- **communist** 名 共産主義者
- **Communist Party** 共産党
- **community** 名 共同社会, 地域社会
- **compact** 名 同意, 協定
- **compensation** 名 補償[賠償]金, 埋め合わせ, 補償
- **competition** 名 競争, 競合, コンペ
- **complain** 動 不平[苦情]を言う
- **complete** 形 完全な, まったくの, 完成した 動 完成させる
- **completion** 名 完成, 完結
- **complex** 形 入り組んだ, 複雑な
- **compromise** 名 妥協, 和解 動 譲歩する, 妥協する
- **concept** 名 ①概念, 観念, テーマ ②(計画案などの)基本的な方向
- **concern** 動 ①関係する,《be -ed in [with] 〜》〜に関係している ②心配させる,《be -ed about [for] 〜》〜を心配する
- **Concord** 名 コンコード(マサチューセッツ州)《町名》
- **condition** 名 条件
- **confederate** 名 連合国
- **Confederate States of America** 南部連合国
- **confederation** 名 同盟, 連合, 連盟
- **conference** 名 ①会議, 協議, 相談 ②協議会
- **conflict** 名 ①不一致, 衝突 ②争い, 対立 ③論争 come into conflict 衝突[対立]する
- **confront** 動 (問題などに)直面する
- **confusion** 名 混乱(状態)
- **Congress** 名 (米国などの)国会, 議会
- **connect** 動 つながる, つなぐ, 関係づける
- **Connecticut River** コネチカット川
- **connection** 名 つながり, 関係
- **consequently** 副 したがって, 結果として
- **conservative** 形 保守的な
- **consider** 動 ①考慮する, 〜しよう

と思う ②(〜と)みなす ③気にかける, 思いやる
- **consist** 動 ①《 – of 〜》(部分・要素から)成る ②《 – in 〜》〜に存在する, 〜にある
- **Constantinople** 名 コンスタンティノープル《東ローマ帝国の首都だったが1453年にオスマン帝国により陥落。現イスタンブール》
- **constitution** 名 憲法, 規約
- **constitutional** 形 憲法の
- **construct** 動 建設する, 組み立てる
- **construction** 名 構造, 建設, 工事, 建物
- **consumer** 名 消費者
- **contain** 動 含む, 入っている
- **continent** 名 大陸
- **continental** 形 大陸の
- **Continental Congress** 大陸会議《英国本国の高圧的な植民地経営に対して北アメリカ13州の自治意識が高まり, 1774年から開催された各植民地代表による会議》
- **continuation** 名 継続, 続行
- **contradiction** 名 否定, 反対
- **control** 動 ①管理[支配]する ②抑制する, コントロールする 名 ①管理, 支配(力) ②抑制 take control of 〜を制御[管理]する, 支配する
- **controversial** 形 論争上の, 議論の余地のある
- **convention** 名 会議, 集会, 大会
- **convince** 動 納得させる, 確信させる
- **cooperation** 名 協力, 協業, 協調
- **corn** 名 トウモロコシ, 穀物
- **corporation** 名 法人, (株式)会社
- **corps** 名 軍団, 部隊
- **corrupt** 形 堕落した, (政治的に)腐敗した
- **corruption** 名 ①堕落 ②腐敗, 汚職
- **cost** 名 ①値段, 費用 ②損失, 犠牲
- **cotton** 名 ①綿, 綿花 ②綿織物, 綿糸
- **cotton gin** 綿繰り機
- **cotton plantation** 綿花プランテーション
- **could** 熟 If +《主語》+ could 〜 できればなあ《仮定法》could have done 〜だったかもしれない《仮定法》
- **council** 名 会議, 評議会, 議会
- **countless** 形 無数の, 数え切れない
- **countryside** 名 地方, 田舎
- **course** 熟 of course もちろん, 当然
- **court** 名 ①中庭, コート ②法廷, 裁判所 ③宮廷, 宮殿
- **cover** 動 補う 名 表紙
- **crash** 動 (事業などが)崩壊する 名 値崩れ, 暴落, 恐慌, 破綻
- **create** 動 創造する, 生み出す, 引き起こす
- **creation** 名 創造[物]
- **creative** 形 創造力のある, 独創的な
- **credit** 名 ①信用, 評判, 名声 ②掛け売り, 信用貸し
- **creditor** 名 債権者, 貸し主
- **crime** 名 ①(法律上の)罪, 犯罪 ②悪事, よくない行為
- **crisis** 名 ①危機, 難局 ②重大局面
- **critical** 形 ①批評の, 批判的な ②危機的な, 重大
- **criticize** 動 ①非難する, あら探しをする ②酷評する ③批判する
- **crop** 名 作物, 収穫
- **crowd** 動 群がる, 混雑する 名 群集, 雑踏, 多数, 聴衆
- **crucial** 形 ①重大な, 決定的な ②

致命的な, 正念場で
- □ **cruel** 形 残酷な, 厳しい
- □ **cruelly** 副 残酷に
- □ **cruelty** 名 残酷さ, 残酷な行為［言動・言葉］
- □ **Cuba** 名 キューバ《国名》
- □ **Cuban** 形 キューバの, キューバ人の
- □ **Cuban Crisis** キューバ危機《1962年10月から11月にかけてキューバに核ミサイル基地の建設が明らかになったことからアメリカ合衆国がカリブ海で海上封鎖を実施し, アメリカ合衆国とソビエト連邦とが対立して緊張が高まり, 全面核戦争前まで達した危機的な状況のこと》
- □ **cultivation** 名 耕作, 栽培, 育成, 養殖
- □ **cultural** 形 文化の, 文化的な
- □ **curious** 形 好奇心の強い, 珍しい, 奇妙な, 知りたがる
- □ **currency** 名 通貨, 貨幣
- □ **current** 形 現在の, 目下の, 通用[流通]している
- □ **cycle** 名 周期, 循環

D

- □ **Dallas** 名 ダラス（テキサス州）《都市名》
- □ **damage** 名 損害, 損傷
- □ **deal** 動 ①分配する ②《–with[in]～》～を扱う 名 ①取引, 扱い ②（不特定の）量, 額 **a good [great] deal (of ～)** かなり［ずいぶん・大量］（の～）, 多額（の～）
- □ **dealt** 動 deal（分配する）の過去, 過去分詞
- □ **death** 名 死, 死ぬこと
- □ **debate** 名 討論, ディベート
- □ **debt** 名 借金, 負債
- □ **decade** 名 10年間
- □ **decision** 名 ①決定, 決心 ②判決
- □ **decision-making** 名 意思［政策・対策］決定
- □ **declaration** 名 ①宣言, 布告 ②告知, 発表
- □ **Declaration of Independence** アメリカ独立宣言《イギリスによって統治されていた北米13の植民地が, 独立したことを宣言する文書。1776年7月4日, 大陸会議によって採択された》
- □ **declare** 動 ①宣言する ②断言する
- □ **decline** 動 衰える
- □ **deeply** 副 深く, 非常に
- □ **defeat** 動 打ち破る, 負かす 名 ①敗北 ②挫折
- □ **defend** 動 防ぐ, 守る, 弁護する
- □ **defense** 名 ①防御, 守備 ②国防
- □ **Delaware** 名 デラウェア州
- □ **Delaware River** デラウェア川《アメリカ合衆国北東部を流れ大西洋に注ぐ川》
- □ **delegate** 名 代表, 代理, 委任
- □ **deletion** 名 削除（部分）
- □ **delivery** 名 配達
- □ **demand** 動 ①要求する, 尋ねる ②必要とする 名 ①要求, 請求 ②需要
- □ **democracy** 名 民主主義, 民主政治
- □ **democrat** 名 民主主義者
- □ **democratic** 形 ①民主主義の, 民主制の ②民主的な
- □ **Democratic National Committee Headquarters** 民主党全国委員会本部
- □ **Democratic Party** 民主党
- □ **Democratic-Republican Party** 民主共和党《アメリカ合衆国の初期の政党。1791-1825》
- □ **demonstration** 名 デモ, 示威運動

WORD LIST

- **denounce** 動 非難する, 告発する
- **densely** 副 密集して
- **departure** 名 離脱
- **depend** 動《- on [upon] ~》①~を頼る, ~をあてにする ②~による
- **dependent** 形 頼っている, ~次第である
- **deploy** 動 (軍隊などを)配備[配置・展開]する
- **deport** 動 (国外に)追放する
- **deposit** 名 鉱床, 鉱脈 placer deposit 砂鉱床
- **depression** 名 不景気, 不況
- **Depression** 名《the -》世界大恐慌《1929～33年の間, 世界中の資本主義諸国を襲った史上最大規模の恐慌》
- **describe** 動 (言葉で)描写する, 特色を述べる, 説明する
- **desire** 名 欲望, 欲求, 願望
- **despite** 前 ~にもかかわらず
- **destiny** 名 運命, 宿命
- **destroy** 動 破壊する, 絶滅させる, 無効にする
- **destruction** 名 破壊(行為・状態)
- **destructive** 形 破壊的な, 有害な
- **détente** 名 (国家間などの)緊張緩和, デタント
- **devastate** 動 荒らす, 荒廃させる, 困惑させる
- **develop** 動 ①発達する[させる] ②開発する
- **development** 名 ①発達, 発展 ②開発
- **device** 名 装置
- **diary** 名 日記
- **dictator** 名 独裁者, 専制者
- **die of** ~がもとで死ぬ
- **diligent** 形 勤勉な, 熱心な, 励んでいる
- **diplomatic** 形 外交(上)の, 外交官の
- **direct** 形 まっすぐな, 直接の, 率直な, 露骨な
- **direction** 名 方向, 方角
- **disability** 名 身体障害
- **disabled** 形《the -》身体障害者
- **disadvantage** 名 不利な立場[条件], 損失
- **disagree** 動 異議を唱える, 反対する
- **disagreement** 名 (意見の)不一致, 相違, 不適合
- **disappear** 動 見えなくなる, 姿を消す, なくなる
- **disappointed** 形 がっかりした, 失望した
- **disaster** 名 災害, 災難, まったくの失敗
- **discrimination** 名 差別, 区別, 識別
- **discussion** 名 討議, 討論
- **disease** 名 病気
- **dispatch** 動 派遣する
- **dissatisfied** 形 不満な, 不満そうな
- **distrust** 名 不信, 疑惑
- **diversity** 名 多様性, 相違
- **divide** 動 分かれる, 分ける, 割れる, 割る divide into ~に分かれる
- **division** 名 ①分割 ②境界
- **doctrine** 名 ①教義, 信条, 主義 ②政策 ③原理, 学説
- **document** 名 文書, 記録 動 (~を)記録する
- **domestically** 副 ①国内で ②家庭的に
- **dominant** 形 支配的な, 優勢な, (遺伝において)優性な
- **Donald Trump** ドナルド・トランプ《第45代アメリカ合衆国大統領(任期2017-)》

A Short History of America

- **double** 動 2倍になる[する]
- **doubt** 名 疑い, 不確かなこと
- **Douglas MacArthur** ダグラス・マッカーサー《アメリカの軍人, 陸軍元帥。連合国軍最高司令官 (1880–1964)》
- **down** 熟 up and down 上がったり下がったり, 行ったり来たり, あちこちと
- **draft** 名 ①下書き, 草稿 ②徴兵招集 動 起草する
- **drastically** 副 大々的に, 徹底的に, 抜本的に, 急激に
- **Dred Scott** ドレッド・スコット《黒人奴隷。スコットは主人に伴われて自由州イリノイや1820年のミズーリ妥協で奴隷制を禁止されたミネソタ準州に住んだことから, 自分とその家族は自由の身になったとして, 1857年2月連邦裁判所に提訴した (c. 1799–1858)》
- **Dred Scott Case** ドレッド・スコット対サンフォード事件《1857年にアメリカ合衆国最高裁判所で下された判決。この判決は, アフリカ人の子孫が奴隷であるか否かに拘らず, アメリカ合衆国の市民にはなれないとし, アメリカ合衆国議会は連邦の領土内で奴隷制を禁じる権限がないとした》
- **drinking** 名 飲むこと, 飲酒
- **drug** 名 麻薬
- **drug cartel** 麻薬カルテル《麻薬の製造・売買に関する活動を行う組織》
- **due** 形 予定された, 期日のきている, 支払われるべき **due to** 〜によって, 〜が原因で
- **Dutch** 形 オランダの 名 オランダ人の
- **Dutch West India Company** オランダ西インド会社《1621年にオランダで設立された貿易会社》
- **duty** 名 ①義務(感), 責任 ②職務, 任務, 関税

- **Dwight D. Eisenhower** ドワイト・D・アイゼンハワー《第34代アメリカ合衆国大統領(任期1953–1961)》

E

- **each other** お互いに
- **ease** 動 楽にする, ゆるめる
- **easily** 副 容易に, たやすく, 苦もなく
- **East Coast** 東海岸, イーストコースト
- **East Germany** ドイツ民主共和国《通称東ドイツ。第二次世界大戦後の1949年に旧ドイツ国のソビエト連邦占領地域に建国された国家 (1949–1990)》
- **eastern** 形 ①東方の, 東向きの ②東洋の, 東洋風の
- **Eastern Europe** 東欧, 東ヨーロッパ
- **economic** 形 経済学の, 経済上の **economic aid** 経済援助 **economic interest** 経済利権
- **Economic and Social Council** 国際連合経済社会理事会《国際連合の主要機関の一つ。経済および社会問題全般に関して必要な議決や勧告等を行う》
- **economically** 副 経済的に, 節約して
- **economy** 名 経済, 財政
- **Edgar Allan Poe** エドガー・アラン・ポー《アメリカ合衆国の小説家, 詩人, 評論家 (1809–1849)》
- **edition** 名 (本・雑誌などの)版
- **education** 名 教育, 教養
- **educational** 形 教育(上)の
- **Edwin E. Aldrin Jr.** バズ・オルドリン《アメリカ航空宇宙局 (NASA) の宇宙飛行士, 空軍軍人。アポロ11号の月着陸船パイロット, 月面歩行を行

WORD LIST

った史上2番目の人類 (1930–)》
- **effect** 名 ①影響, 効果, 結果 ②実施, 発効 put ~ into effect (法律など) の発効を命ずる
- **effort** 名 努力 (の成果)
- **Egypt** 名 エジプト《国名》
- **elderly** 名《the –》お年寄り
- **elect** 動 選ぶ, (~することに)決める, 選挙する
- **election** 名 選挙, 投票
- **elector** 名 選挙人, 有権者
- **electoral** 形 選挙の
- **Electoral College** アメリカ選挙人団《アメリカ合衆国大統領選挙の選挙人集会で大統領及び副大統領を選出する選挙人の集合》
- **electrical** 形 電気の, 電気に関する
- **electronic** 形 電子工学の, エレクトロニクスの
- **electronics** 名 エレクトロニクス, 電子工学, 電子機器
- **Elvis Presley** エルヴィス・プレスリー《アメリカのミュージシャン, 映画俳優。ロックンロールの創始者の一人 (1935–1977)》
- **emancipation** 名 (政治的・社会的な束縛や圧迫からの) 解放
- **Emancipation Proclamation** 奴隷解放宣言《アメリカ合衆国大統領であったエイブラハム・リンカーンが, 南北戦争中の1862年9月, 南部連合が支配する地域の奴隷たちの解放を命じた宣言》
- **embarkation** 名 乗船
- **embassy** 名 大使館
- **emergency** 名 非常時, 緊急時 形 緊急の emergency measures 応急手段
- **emigrant** 名 (他国への)移民, 移住者
- **Emigrant Trail** 移民街道《19世紀, 北アメリカ大陸の西部開拓時代にアメリカ合衆国の開拓者達が通った主要道の総称》
- **Emilio Aguinaldo** エミリオ・アギナルド《フィリピンの革命家。フィリピン第一共和国の初代大統領 (任期 1899–1901)》
- **emperor** 名 皇帝, 天皇
- **empire** 名 帝国
- **employee** 名 従業員, 会社員, 被雇用者
- **employment** 名 ①雇用 ②仕事, 職
- **encourage** 動 ①勇気づける ②促進する, 助長する
- **end** 熟 at the end of ~の終わりに bring to an end 終わらせる, ピリオドを打つ in the end 結局
- **enemy** 名 敵
- **enforce** 動 (法律などを)実行する, 実施する, 施行する
- **England** 名 ①イングランド ②英国
- **Englishman** 名 イングランド人, イギリス人
- **enormous** 形 ばく大な, 非常に大きい, 巨大な
- **enter into** ~に入る
- **enterprise** 名 ①企業, 事業 ②計画, 活動
- **entire** 形 全体の, 完全な, まったくの
- **entrepreneur** 名 企業家, 起業家
- **environment** 名 ①環境 ②周囲 (の状況), 情勢
- **environmental** 形 ①環境の, 周囲の ②環境保護の
- **epilogue** 名 ①(劇の)納め口上, エピローグ ②終章, 終節
- **equal** 形 等しい, 均等な, 平等な
- **equality** 名 平等, 等しいこと
- **equally** 副 等しく, 平等に
- **era** 名 時代, 年代

A Short History of America

- **Erie Canal** エリー運河《米ニューヨーク州のハドソン川からエリー湖までをつなぐ約584kmの運河》
- **Erie, Lake** エリー湖《五大湖の一つ》
- **escalate** 動 段階的に増大する，エスカレートする
- **escape** 動 逃げる，免れる，もれる
- **essential** 形 本質的な，必須の
- **establish** 動 確立する，立証する，設置［設立］する
- **establishment** 名 確立，設立，発足
- **estate** 名 不動産，財産，遺産，地所，土地 real estate 不動産，土地
- **Eurasia** 名 ユーラシア（大陸）
- **Europe** 名 ヨーロッパ
- **European** 名 ヨーロッパ人 形 ヨーロッパ（人）の
- **European Settlement** ヨーロッパ人の入植
- **even if** たとえ～でも
- **even though** ～であるけれども，～にもかかわらず
- **eventually** 副 結局は
- **everybody** 代 誰でも，皆
- **everyday** 形 毎日の，日々の
- **everything** 代 すべてのこと［もの］，何でも，何もかも
- **everywhere** 副 どこにいても，いたるところに
- **evidence** 名 ①証拠，証人 ②形跡
- **evolve** 動 進化する［させる］，発展する［させる］
- **example** 熟 for example たとえば
- **excellent** 形 優れた，優秀な
- **except** 前 ～を除いて，～のほかは except for ～を除いて，～がなければ
- **exception** 名 例外，除外，異論

- **executive** 名 ①高官，実行委員 ②重役，役員，幹部
- **exhaust** 動 ①ひどく疲れさせる ②使い果たす
- **exile** 名 追放（者），亡命（者）
- **exist** 動 存在する，生存する，ある，いる
- **expand** 動 ①広げる，拡張［拡大］する ②発展させる，拡充する
- **expansion** 名 拡大，拡張，展開
- **expect** 動 予期［予測］する，(当然のこととして)期待する
- **experienced** 形 経験のある，経験を積んだ
- **experimental** 形 実験の，試験的な
- **expertise** 名 専門知識［技術］
- **explore** 動 探検［調査］する，切り開く
- **explorer** 名 探検者［家］
- **explosion** 名 爆発
- **export** 動 輸出する 名 輸出，国外への持ち出し
- **exportable** 形 輸出可能な，輸出向きの
- **exposed** 形 雨風［光，攻撃，危険］にさらされた
- **exposition** 名 博覧会
- **express** 動 表現する，述べる
- **extinct** 形 消えた，絶滅した
- **extinction** 名 絶滅，死滅
- **extraordinarily** 副 異常に，並はずれて，法外に

F

- **fabric** 名 ①織物，生地 ②構造
- **fact** 熟 in fact つまり，実は，要するに
- **factor** 名 要因，要素，因子

Word List

- **factory** 名 工場, 製造所
- **fail** 動 ①失敗する, 落第する［させる］②《－to ～》～し損なう, ～できない
- **failure** 名 ①失敗, 落第 ②不足, 欠乏 ③停止, 減退
- **fair** 形 正しい, 公平［正当］な
- **Fair Deal** フェア・ディール《ハリー・S・トルーマン米国大統領が1949年1月の一般教書にてアメリカ合衆国議会に示した, 一連の提案に与えられた名称。「公正な扱い」の意》
- **fall behind** 取り残される, 後れを取る
- **fall into** ～に陥る, ～してしまう
- **fallen** 動 fall（落ちる）の過去分詞
- **Falmouth** 名 ファルマス《マサチューセッツ州の港町》
- **famously** 副 よく知られているように, 周知のとおり
- **fanatic** 形 狂信的な, 熱狂的な
- **Far East** 極東, ファーイースト
- **farewell** 名 別れ, 別れのあいさつ
- **farming** 名 農業, 農作業
- **fear** 動 ①恐れる ②心配する
- **federal** 形 連邦政府の, 連邦の
- **Federal Republic of Germany** ドイツ連邦共和国
- **Federal Reserve System** 連邦準備制度《アメリカ合衆国の中央銀行制度》
- **Federal Trade Commission** 連邦取引委員会《アメリカ合衆国における公正な取引を監督・監視する連邦政府の機関》
- **federalism** 名 （政治体制の）連邦主義
- **Federalist Party** 連邦党《強力な連邦政府樹立を目指したアメリカの政党。1787年結成》
- **female** 形 女性の, 婦人の, 雌の 名 婦人, 雌
- **Fidel Castro** フィデル・カストロ《キューバの政治家, 革命家, 軍人（1926–2016）》
- **fierce** 形 どう猛な, 荒々しい, すさまじい, 猛烈な
- **fiercely** 副 どう猛に, 猛烈に
- **fight back** 反撃に転じる, 応戦する
- **fighter** 名 ①戦士 ②戦闘機
- **fighting** 名 戦闘
- **Filipino** 形 フィリピン人の
- **final** 形 最後の, 決定的な
- **financial** 形 ①財務（上）の, 金融（上）の ②金融関係者の
- **financially** 副 財政的に, 金銭的に
- **first** 熟 at first 最初のうちは first of all まず第一に
- **First World War** 第一次世界大戦《1914年7月28日から1918年11月11日にかけて, 連合国対中央同盟国の戦闘により繰り広げられた世界大戦》
- **fix** 動 ①固定する［させる］②修理する ③決定する ④用意する, 整える
- **flame** 名 炎, （炎のような）輝き
- **flavor** 名 風味, 味わい, 趣
- **fled** 動 flee（逃げる）の過去, 過去分詞
- **flight** 名 飛ぶこと, 飛行, （飛行機の）フライト
- **Florida** 名 フロリダ州
- **flour** 名 小麦粉
- **focus** 動 ①焦点を合わせる ②（関心・注意を）集中させる
- **followed by** その後に～が続いて
- **follower** 名 信奉者, 追随者
- **following** 形 《the －》次の, 次に続く 名 《the －》下記のもの, 以下に述べるもの
- **force** 名 力, 勢い 動 ①強制する, 力ずくで～する, 余儀なく～させる ②押しやる, 押し込む

- **Ford Model T** フォード・モデルT《フォード・モーター社が開発・製造した自動車 (1908-1927)》
- **Ford Motor Company** フォード・モーター・カンパニー《アメリカの自動車メーカー (1903年設立)》
- **Ford Thunderbird** フォード・サンダーバード《フォード社製のスペシャリティー・カー》
- **foreign affairs** 外務
- **foreign aid** 対外援助
- **form** 名 形, 形式 動 形づくる
- **formal** 形 正式の, 公式の, 形式的な, 格式ばった
- **former** 形 ①前の, 先の, 以前の ②《the-》(二者のうち) 前者の
- **formerly** 副 元は, 以前は
- **fort** 名 砦, 要塞
- **Fort Sumter** サムター要塞《サウスカロライナ州チャールストンの港に位置する石造りの要塞》
- **Fort Sumter, Battle of** サムター要塞の戦い《1861年4月12日から4月14日にかけて行なわれた戦闘。南北戦争の発端とされる戦い》
- **Fort Ticonderoga** タイコンデロガ砦《ニューヨーク州ハドソン川峡谷にあるシャンプレーン湖の細くなった南端にある大きな砦》
- **fortune** 名 富, 財産
- **founder** 名 創立者, 設立者
- **Fourteen Points** 十四か条の平和原則《1918年1月8日, アメリカ大統領ウッドロウ・ウィルソンが, アメリカ連邦議会での演説のなかで発表した平和原則》
- **Fourteenth Amendment** アメリカ合衆国憲法第14条《南北戦争後に成立した憲法修正条項の1つ》
- **France** 名 フランス《国名》
- **frank** 形 率直な, 隠し立てをしない
- **Franklin D. Roosevelt** フランクリン・ルーズベルト《第32代アメリカ合衆国大統領 (1933-1945)》
- **fraud** 名 詐欺, 詐欺師
- **freedman** 名 (奴隷から解放された) 自由民
- **Freedmen's Bureau** 解放黒人局《南北戦争によって解放された黒人を保護するために設けられたアメリカの連邦部局 (1865-1872)》
- **Freedmen's Bureau Act** 解放黒人局延長法案
- **freedom** 名 ①自由 ②束縛がないこと **freedom of the press** 出版 [報道・言論] の自由
- **freely** 副 自由に, 障害なしに
- **French** 形 フランス (人・語) の 名 ①フランス語 ②《the-》フランス人
- **French and Indian War** フレンチ・インディアン戦争《七年戦争に関連し, 北米植民地で戦われた, フランス・インディアン連合軍とイギリスとの戦争 (1754-1763)》
- **French-Canadian fort** フレンチ・カナディアン要塞《フレンチ・インディアン戦争当時, フランス軍がオハイオ川上流に築いた要塞》
- **Frenchman** 名 フランス人の男, フランス人
- **frequently** 副 頻繁に, しばしば
- **frontier** 名 国境, 辺境, フロンティア
- **frozen** 形 ①凍った ②冷淡な
- **frustrated** 形 挫折した, 失望した
- **frustration** 名 欲求不満, 失意, 挫折
- **fugitive** 形 逃亡中の
- **Fugitive Slave Act** 逃亡奴隷法《逃亡した黒人奴隷を所有者に返すことを規定したアメリカの法律。1793年と1850年にアメリカ議会で制定された》
- **full of** 《be-》〜で一杯である
- **fully** 副 十分に, 完全に, まるまる

WORD LIST

- **fundamental** 形 基本の, 根本的な, 重要な
- **Fundamental Orders** 基本的秩序《コネチカット植民地で制定された, 北アメリカで最初の憲法と考えられている文書(1639)》
- **fur** 名 毛, 毛皮(製品)
- **furious** 形 怒り狂った, 激怒した, 激しい
- **further** 形 いっそう遠い, その上の, なおいっそうの 副 いっそう遠く, その上に, もっと
- **furthermore** 副 さらに, その上
- **future** 熟 in the future 将来は

G

- **gain** 動 ①得る, 増す ②進歩する, 進む
- **gap** 名 ギャップ, 隔たり, すき間
- **gas** 名 (燃料用) ガス
- **gasoline** 名 ガソリン
- **gather** 動 集まる, 集める
- **general** 形 ①全体の, 一般の, 普通の ②おおよその ③(職位の)高い, 上級の 名 大将, 将軍
- **generally** 副 ①一般に, だいたい ②たいてい
- **generation** 名 ①同世代の人々 ②一世代 ③発生, 生成
- **George H. W. Bush** ジョージ・H・W・ブッシュ《第41代アメリカ合衆国大統領(任期1989–1993)》
- **George III, King** ジョージ3世《イギリス国王(1738–1820)》
- **George W. Bush** ジョージ・W・ブッシュ《第43代アメリカ合衆国大統領(任期2001–2009)》
- **George Washington** ジョージ・ワシントン《初代アメリカ合衆国大統領(任期1789–1797)》
- **Georgia** 名 ジョージア州
- **Gerald R. Ford** ジェラルド・R・フォード《第38代アメリカ合衆国大統領(任期1974–1977)》
- **German** 形 ドイツ(人・語)の 名 ①ドイツ人 ②ドイツ語
- **German Democratic Republic** ドイツ民主共和国《通称東ドイツ。第二次世界大戦後の1949年に旧ドイツ国のソビエト連邦占領地域に建国された国家(1949–1990)》
- **Germany** 名 ドイツ《国名》
- **get someone to do** (人)に〜させる[してもらう]
- **get to** 〜に達する[到着する]
- **get used to** 〜になじむ, 〜に慣れる
- **Gettysburg, Battle of** ゲティスバーグの戦い《南北戦争において事実上の決戦となった戦い(1863)》
- **Ghent, Treaty of** ガン条約《米英戦争の講和条約で, 1814年12月に南ネーデルラント(ベルギー)のヘント(ガン)で結ばれた》
- **giant** 形 巨大な, 偉大な
- **gin** 名 《cotton –》綿繰り機, ジン
- **give rise to** 〜を引き起こす
- **give up** あきらめる, やめる, 引き渡す
- **global** 形 地球(上)の, 地球規模の, 世界的な, 国際的な
- **Global warming** 地球温暖化
- **go out into** 〜に出て行く
- **gold** 名 金, 金貨, 金製品, 金色
- **golden** 形 ①金色の ②金製の ③貴重な
- **goods** 名 ①商品, 品物 ②財産, 所有物
- **Google** 名 グーグル《インターネット関連のサービスと製品に特化したアメリカの多国籍テクノロジー企業》
- **Gorbachev** 名 ミハイル・ゴルバチョフ《ソビエト連邦第8代最高指導者(任期1985–1991)》

- **Gouverneur Morris** ガバヌーア・モリス《アメリカ合衆国の政治家。1787年合衆国憲法制定会議では最終案を執筆 (1752–1816)》
- **govern** 動 治める、管理する
- **government** 名 政治、政府、支配
- **governor** 名 知事
- **gradually** 副 だんだんと
- **grant** 動 ①許可する、承諾する ②授与する、譲渡する
- **grave** 名 墓
- **Great Boston Fire of 1871** ボストン大火《1872年11月9日夜に起こったボストンの歴史上最大の大火》
- **Great Chicago Fire** シカゴ大火《1871年10月8日夜にイリノイ州シカゴ市内で発生した大規模火災》
- **great deal of** 《a –》多量の、大量の
- **Great Lakes** 五大湖《アメリカ合衆国及びカナダの国境付近に連なる5つの湖の総称。スペリオル湖、ミシガン湖、ヒューロン湖、エリー湖、オンタリオ湖の5つの湖からなる》
- **Great Society** 偉大な社会《リンドン・ジョンソン第36代大統領が1965年に提唱した社会福祉政策》
- **greatly** 副 大いに
- **Grover Cleveland** グロバー・クリーブランド《第22代および第24代アメリカ合衆国大統領 (任期1885–1889、1893–1897)》
- **growth** 名 成長、発展
- **Guadalcanal** ガタルカナル島《ソロモン諸島最大の島。第二次世界大戦の激戦地》
- **Guadalupe Hidalgo, Treaty of** グアダルーペ・イダルゴ条約《米墨戦争 (1846–1848) を終結させた1848年5月の条約》
- **Guam** 名 グアム《太平洋にあるマリアナ諸島南端の島》
- **guerrilla** 名 ゲリラ兵
- **guidance** 名 案内、手引き、指導
- **guilty** 形 有罪の、やましい
- **gulf** 名 湾
- **Gulf of Mexico** メキシコ湾
- **Gulf War** 湾岸戦争《1990年8月2日、イラクによるクウェート侵攻をきっかけとした国際紛争 (1991)》
- **gunboat** 名 小砲艦《小型の沿岸警備艇》

H

- **Half Moon** ハーフムーン号《ヘンリー・ハドソンが1609年、大西洋横断航海に出た時の船》
- **Halsey** ウィリアム・ハルゼー・ジュニア《アメリカ合衆国の海軍軍人 (1882–1959)》
- **Hampton Roads, Battle of** ハンプトン・ローズ海戦《南北戦争中に生起した海戦。鉄板で装甲された動力軍艦同士の歴史上最初の戦い (1862)》
- **hand** 熟 hand over 手渡す、引き渡す、譲渡する on the other hand 一方、他方では
- **happiness** 名 幸せ、喜び
- **harbor** 名 港、停泊所、隠れ場
- **hard time** 《a –》つらい時期
- **hardship** 名 (耐えがたい) 苦難、辛苦
- **harmoniously** 副 平和に
- **Harriet Beecher Stowe** ハリエット・ビーチャー・ストウ《アメリカ合衆国の奴隷制廃止論者、作家 (1811–1896)》
- **Harry S. Truman** ハリー・S・トルーマン《第33代アメリカ合衆国大統領 (任期1945–1953)》
- **harvest** 動 収穫する
- **Hawaii** 名 ハワイ《米国の州》
- **Head Start** ヘッドスタート《社会

的に不利益を蒙っている就学前の子供たちのニーズに応えようとするプログラム。リンドン・ジョンソン大統領の「貧困との戦い」キャンペーンの一部として始められたもの》

- **headquarters** 名 本部, 司令部, 本署
- **heal** 動 いえる, いやす, 治る, 治す
- **health care** 健康保険制度
- **heat** 名 熱, 暑さ　heat wave 熱波
- **heavy industry** 重工業
- **height** 名 高台, 丘
- **Henry Clay** ヘンリー・クレイ《アメリカ合衆国の政治家であり雄弁家, ホイッグ党の創設者かつ指導者 (1777-1852)》
- **Henry Hudson** ヘンリー・ハドソン《イングランドの航海士, 探検家。北アメリカ東海岸やカナダ北東部を探検した (1560～70頃-1611?)》
- **Henry Wadsworth Longfellow** ヘンリー・ワーズワース・ロングフェロー《アメリカ合衆国の詩人 (1807-1882)》
- **Hernán Cortés** エルナン・コルテス《スペインのコンキスタドール。メキシコ高原にあったアステカ帝国を征服した (1485-1547)》
- **herd** 名 (大型動物の)一群, 群集
- **Hernando de Soto** エルナンド・デ・ソト《スペイン人探検家でコンキスタドール。現在のアメリカ合衆国の領地へ最初の白人の遠征隊を率いて, ミシシッピ川を白人として最初に発見した (1496または1497-1542)》
- **hesitate** 動 ためらう, ちゅうちょする
- **highlight** 動 注目させる, 強調する
- **hijack** 動 ハイジャックする, 乗っ取る
- **Hilary Clinton** ヒラリー・クリントン《アメリカ合衆国の政治家, 弁護士 (1947-)》

- **historic** 形 歴史上有名 [重要] な, 歴史的な
- **hit back at** ～に対抗する
- **home** 熟 at home 自宅で, 在宅して, 自国で
- **honor** 名 ①名誉, 光栄, 信用 ②節操, 自尊心　in honor of ～に敬意を表して, ～を祝って, ～を記念して
- **Hoover** ハーバート・フーヴァー《第31代アメリカ合衆国大統領 (任期1929-1933)》
- **hope** 熟 in the hope of ～を望んで [期待して]
- **House Minority Leader** 下院少数党内総務
- **housing** 名 住宅供給, 住居, 家
- **how to** ～する方法
- **Howe** ウィリアム・ハウ《イギリス軍の将軍, アメリカ独立戦争の時はイギリス軍の総司令官 (1729-1814)》
- **however** 副 たとえ～でも 接 けれども, だが
- **Hudson River** ハドソン川《アメリカ合衆国の主にニューヨーク州を流れ, 大西洋に注ぐ川》
- **huge** 形 巨大な, ばく大な
- **human being** 人, 人間
- **hundreds of** 何百もの～
- **hunt** 動 狩る, 狩りをする

I

- **ideal** 名 理想, 究極の目標
- **if** 接 If + 《主語》+ could ～できればなあ《仮定法》　as if あたかも～のように, まるで～みたいに　even if たとえ～でも　see if ～かどうかを確かめる
- **ignore** 動 無視する, 怠る
- **illegal** 形 違法な, 不法な
- **illegally** 副 違法に, 不法に

A Short History of America

- **Illinois** 名 イリノイ州
- **immediate** 形 さっそくの, 即座の, 直接の
- **immediately** 副 すぐに, ～するやいなや
- **immigrant** 名 移民, 移住者 形 移民に関する
- **immigrate** 動 (他国から)移住する, 移住させる
- **immigration** 名 ①移民局, 入国管理 ②移住, 入植
- **Imperial Japanese Navy** 大日本帝国海軍
- **import** 動 輸入する 名 輸入, 輸入品
- **importance** 名 重要性, 大切さ
- **importantly** 副 重大に, もったいぶって
- **imported** 形 輸入された
- **impose** 動 課す, 負わせる, 押しつける
- **impress** 動 印象づける, 感銘させる
- **improve** 動 改善する[させる], 進歩する
- **improvement** 名 改良, 改善
- **incident** 名 出来事, 事故, 事変, 紛争
- **include** 動 含む, 勘定に入れる
- **including** 前 ～を含めて, 込みで
- **increase** 動 増加[増強]する, 増やす, 増える 名 増加(量), 増大
- **increasing** 形 増加する, 拡大する
- **independence** 名 独立心, 自立
- **independent** 形 独立した, 自立した
- **India** 名 インド《国名》
- **Indian** 名 ①インド人 ②(アメリカ)インディアン 形 ①インド(人)の ②(アメリカ)インディアンの
- **Indiana** 名 インディアナ州
- **Indies** 名 インド諸国《インド・インドシナ・東インド諸島の総称的旧名》
- **indigo** 名 インディゴ, 藍《染料》
- **industrial** 形 工業の, 産業の
- **industry** 名 産業, 工業
- **inflation** 名 ①膨張 ②インフレーション《物価の暴騰》
- **influence** 名 影響, 勢力 動 影響をおよぼす
- **influential** 形 影響力の大きい, 有力な
- **ingenious** 形 発明の才のある, 独創的な
- **inland** 形 ①内陸の, 奥地の ②国内の, 内地の
- **innocent** 形 無邪気な, 無実の
- **innovation** 名 ①革新, 刷新 ②新しいもの, 新考案
- **innovative** 形 革新的な, 創造力に富む
- **insist** 動 ①主張する, 断言する ②要求する
- **instantly** 副 すぐに, 即座に
- **instead** 副 その代わりに
- **intelligence** 名 ①知能 ②情報
- **intend** 動《 – to ～》～しようと思う, ～するつもりである
- **intense** 形 ①強烈な, 激しい ②感情的な
- **interest** 名 利権
- **interested** 形 興味を持った, 関心のある
- **internally** 副 ①内部に ②内面的に, 精神的に ③国内に
- **International Court of Justice** 国際司法裁判所《国際連合の主要機関のひとつ》
- **internationally** 形 国際的に
- **invade** 動 侵入する, 攻め入る
- **invader** 名 侵入者, 侵略国, 侵略軍

WORD LIST

- **invasion** 名 侵略, 侵害
- **invent** 動 発明[考案]する
- **invention** 名 発明(品)
- **inventor** 名 発明者, 発案者
- **invest** 動 投資する,(金・精力などを)注ぐ
- **investment** 名 投資, 出資
- **investor** 名 出資者, 投資家
- **involve** 動 ①含む, 伴う ②巻き込む, かかわらせる
- **involved** 形 ①巻き込まれている, 関連する ②入り組んだ, 込み入っている
- **involvement** 名 関与
- **Iowa** 名 アイオワ州
- **Iran** 名 イラン《国名》
- **Iranian Revolution** イラン革命《1978年にシーア派のホメイニらを指導者として勃発し, 翌年, 独裁政権パフラビー王朝を倒したイランの革命》
- **Iraq** 名 イラク《国名》
- **Iraqi** 形 イラク(人)の
- **iron** 名 鉄, 鉄製のもの 形 鉄の, 鉄製の
- **ironclad** 形 (戦艦などが)装甲した
- **Iroquois** 名 イロコイ・インディアン, イロコイ連合《イロコイ語の北米インディアン(今のニューヨークからナイアガラ滝までの一帯の)》
- **Iroquois Five Nations** イロコイ連合《17世紀, 互いに戦争状態にあった五大湖畔のカユーガ族, モホーク族, オナイダ族, オノンダーガ族, セネカ族の5つの部族の同盟。18世紀前半にタスカローラ族が加わり6部族連合となる》
- **Islamic** 形 イスラムの, イスラム教の
- **Islamic State** イスラム国, ISIS《イスラム国家の樹立を掲げてイラクやシリアで活動するスンニ派の武装勢力》
- **Israel** 名 イスラエル《国名》
- **issue** 名 ①問題, 論点 ②発行物 ③出口, 流出 動 ①(~から)出る, 生じる ②発行する
- **Isthmus of Panama** パナマ地峡《中央アメリカのカリブ海と太平洋との間, パナマ中部にあり, 南北アメリカ大陸を結ぶ帯状の地峡》
- **Italian** 形 イタリア(人・語)の 名 ①イタリア人 ②イタリア語
- **Italy** 名 イタリア《国名》
- **itself** 代 それ自体, それ自身
- **Iwo-Jima** 名 硫黄島《小笠原諸島の南端近くに所在する、東西8 km, 南北4 kmの島。太平洋戦争(第二次世界大戦)の激戦地として知られる》

J

- **Jacksonian Democracy** ジャクソン流民主主義《アメリカ合衆国の大統領アンドリュー・ジャクソンとその支持者の政治哲学のこと》
- **Jacques Cartier** ジャック・カルティエ《フランス, サン・マロ出身のブルトン人探検家。北米大陸へ3度の探検を行い, 後のフランスによるカナダ領有の基礎を築いた(1491-1557)》
- **James Buchanan** ジェームズ・ブキャナン《第15代アメリカ合衆国大統領(任期1857-1861)》
- **James E. Carter** ジミー・カーター《第39代アメリカ合衆国大統領(任期1977-1981)》
- **James I, King** ジェームズ1世《スコットランド王/イングランド王(1566-1625)》
- **James K. Polk** ジェームズ・ポーク《第11代アメリカ合衆国大統領(任期1845-1849)》
- **James Madison** ジェームズ・マディソン《第4代アメリカ合衆国大統領(任期1809-1817)》

A SHORT HISTORY OF AMERICA

- **James Monroe** ジェームズ・モンロー《第5代アメリカ合衆国大統領(任期1817–1825)》
- **James Otis** ジェイムズ・オーティス《マサチューセッツ湾直轄植民地の法律家, 政治活動家。「代表なき課税は暴政である」というフレーズを初めて使ったとされる(1725–1783)》
- **Jamestown** 名 ジェームズタウン(バージニア州)《イギリスが北アメリカに建設した最初の永続的植民地》
- **Japan** 名 日本《国名》
- **Japanese** 形 日本(人・語)の 名 ①日本人 ②日本語
- **jazz** 名 ジャズ
- **Jazz Age** ジャズ・エイジ《狂騒の20年代と呼ばれるアメリカ合衆国の1920年代の文化・世相を指す言葉。F・スコット・フィッツジェラルドの『ジャズ・エイジの物語』(1922年)に由来》
- **Jefferson Davis** ジェファーソン・デイヴィス《アメリカ連合国大統領(任期1861–1865)》
- **Jeremiah Dixon** ジェレマイア・ディクソン《イギリスの測地学者, 天文学者。1763年から1767年にわたって, チャールズ・メイソンとともに, ペンシルベニア植民地とメリーランド植民地との境界線を確定したメイソン=ディクソン線の測量をおこなった(1733–1779)》
- **Jesus** 名 イエス・キリスト《キリスト教の始祖(前4頃–30頃)》
- **Jew** 名 ユダヤ人
- **Jim Crow laws** ジム・クロウ法《1876年から1964年にかけて存在した, 人種差別的内容を含むアメリカ合衆国南部諸州の州法の総称》
- **John Adams** ジョン・アダムス《第2代アメリカ合衆国大統領(任期1797–1801)》
- **John Cabot** ジョン・カボット《中世の航海者。カトリック教徒。北アメリカ大陸の発見者として知られる(1450頃–1498)》
- **John F. Kennedy** ジョン・F・ケネディ《第35代アメリカ合衆国大統領(任期1961–1963)》
- **John Hancock** ジョン・ハンコック《アメリカ合衆国の政治家。アメリカ独立宣言に最初に署名した(1736–1793)》
- **John L. O'Sullivan** ジョン・オサリヴァン《アメリカ合衆国のコラムニスト, 編集者である。テキサス併合とオレゴン・カントリーの境界線引きが問題になっていた1845年に, アメリカ合衆国の西方拡張を正当化する「マニフェスト・デスティニー」という表現を最初に用いた人物》
- **John Quincy Adams** ジョン・クィンシー・アダムズ《第6代アメリカ合衆国大統領(任期1825–1829)》
- **John Smith** ジョン・スミス《イギリスの軍人, 植民請負人。ジェームズタウンを建設した(1580–1631)》
- **John Tyler** ジョン・タイラー《第10代アメリカ合衆国大統領(任期1841–1845)》
- **join in** 加わる, 参加する
- **joint** 形 共同の, ジョイントした
- **journey** 名 ①(遠い目的地への)旅 ②行程
- **joy** 名 喜び, 楽しみ
- **jungle** 名 ジャングル, 入り組んだもの
- **just as** (ちょうど)であろうとおり
- **justice** 名 ①公平, 公正, 正当, 正義 ②司法, 裁判(官)
- **justify** 動 正しいとする, 弁明する

K

- **Kansas** 名 カンザス州
- **Kansas–Nebraska Act** カンザス・ネブラスカ法《1854年, カンザス及びネブラスカ両准州を設立する法

Word List

- 律。ミズーリ協定を否定し、準州が州昇格の際に自由州か奴隷州かを住民が選択できるとした》
- **Kentucky** 名ケンタッキー州
- **King William's War** ウィリアム王戦争《1689年から97年にかけて北アメリカ植民地で戦われたイギリスとフランスとの戦争》
- **kingdom** 名王国
- **knowledge** 名知識、理解、学問
- **known as** 《be –》～として知られている
- **Korea** 名朝鮮、大韓民国(韓国)
- **Korean** 形韓国(人・語)の、朝鮮(人・語)の 名①韓国[朝鮮]人 ②韓国[朝鮮]語
- **Korean Peninsula** 朝鮮半島
- **Korean War** 朝鮮戦争《大韓民国(韓国)と朝鮮民主主義人民共和国(北朝鮮)の間で生じた朝鮮半島の主権を巡る国際紛争(1950–1953)》
- **Ku Klux Klan** クー・クラックス・クラン《アメリカの秘密結社。白人至上主義団体。略称KKK(1865設立)》
- **Kum River** 錦江《大韓民国南西部の主要河川》
- **Kuwait** 名クウェート《国名》

L

- **labor** 名労働、骨折り
- **Labor Management Relations Act of 1947** 1947年労使関係法《労働組合の活動と勢力を監視する米国連邦法。通称タフト＝ハートリー法》
- **laborer** 名労働者
- **laid** 動 lay (置く)の過去、過去分詞
- **Lake Erie** エリー湖
- **landing** 名上陸
- **landowner** 名地主
- **large-wheeled wagon** 大きな車輪をもった荷馬車
- **Latin** 名①ラテン語 ②ラテン系民族の人 形ラテン(語・系)の
- **launch** 動①(ロケットなどを)打ち上げる、発射する ②進水させる ③(事業などを)始める
- **law-making** 形立法の
- **lawyer** 名弁護士、法律家
- **lead to** ～に至る、～に通じる、～を引き起こす
- **leadership** 名指揮、リーダーシップ
- **league** 名①同盟、連盟 ②(スポーツの)競技連盟
- **League of Nations** 国際連盟《第一次大戦後、国際間の協力によって国際平和を維持するため、米国大統領ウィルソンの提唱によって1920年に設立された国際機関》
- **leap** 動①跳ぶ ②跳び越える
- **leave ~ for ...** ～を発って…に向かう
- **led** 動 lead (導く)の過去、過去分詞
- **legal** 形法律(上)の、正当な
- **Lehman Brothers** リーマン・ブラザーズ《かつてアメリカのニューヨークに本社を置いていた大手投資銀行グループ》
- **lend** 動貸す、貸し出す
- **length** 名長さ、縦、たけ、距離
- **Leon Czolgosz** レオン・チョルゴッシュ《アメリカ合衆国の無政府主義者。ウィリアム・マッキンリー大統領を暗殺した事で知られる(1873–1901)》
- **Leonid Brezhnev** レオニード・ブレジネフ《ソビエト連邦第5代最高指導者。(任期1964–1982)》
- **less** 形～より小さい[少ない] 副～より少なく、～ほどでなく
- **level** 名①水平、平面 ②水準

A Short History of America

- **Lexington** 名 レキシントン（ケンタッキー州）《地名》
- **Lexington and Concord, Battle of** レキシントン・コンコードの戦い《1775年4月19日に起こった、アメリカ独立戦争が始まる契機となった英米間の戦闘》
- **liberal** 形 ①自由主義の, 進歩的な ②気前のよい 名 ①自由主義者
- **liberty** 名 ①自由, 解放 ②《-ties》特権, 特典 ③《-ties》勝手な振る舞い
- **lie** 動 （ある状態に）ある, 存在する
- **Lieutenant General** 中将
- **life** 熟 way of life 生き様, 生き方, 暮らし方
- **lifestyle** 名 生活様式, ライフスタイル
- **light bulb** 電球
- **limit** 名 限界,《-s》範囲, 境界 動 制限[限定]する
- **limitation** 名 制限, 限度
- **link** 動 連結する, つながる
- **liquor** 名 （強い）酒
- **literary** 形 文学の, 文芸の
- **literature** 名 文学, 文芸
- **Little Rock** リトルロック（アーカンソー州）《地名》
- **living** 名 生計, 生活
- **locate** 動 置く
- **Long Island, Battle of** ロングアイランドの戦い《1776年8月22日から同年8月30日にかけて、現在のニューヨーク市ブルックリンを主戦場にして戦われた、アメリカ独立戦争の主要な戦闘のひとつ》
- **long-lasting** 形 長続きする, 長持ちする
- **longer** 熟 no longer もはや～でない[～しない]
- **loosely** 副 ①ゆるく, おおざっぱに ②だらしなく
- **lord** 名 ①首長, 主人, 領主, 貴族, 上院議員
- **Lord North** フレデリック・ノース（ノース卿）《イギリスの政治家, 貴族。1770年から1782年まで首相を務めたが, 在任期間の後半はアメリカ独立戦争への対応に追われた（1732–1792）》
- **loss** 名 ①損失（額・物）, 損害, 浪費 ②失敗, 敗北
- **Louis XIV** ルイ14世《フランス国王（在位1643–1715）》
- **Louisiana** 名 ルイジアナ州
- **Louisiana Territory** ルイジアナ準州
- **lower** 形 もっと低い, 下級の, 劣った
- **lynch** 動 （人）を私刑によって殺す
- **Lyndon B. Johnson** リンドン・ジョンソン《第36代アメリカ合衆国大統領（任期1963–1969）》

M

- **main** 形 主な, 主要な
- **Maine** 名 メイン州
- **mainly** 副 主に
- **maintain** 動 ①維持する ②養う
- **major** 形 大きいほうの, 主な
- **majority** 名 ①大多数, 大部分 ②過半数
- **make money** お金を儲ける
- **make progress** 進歩[上達]する, 前進する
- **make the most of** ～を最大限利用する
- **making** 名 制作, 製造
- **Malcolm X** マルコム・X《アメリカの黒人公民権運動活動家。アメリカで最も著名で攻撃的な黒人解放指導者として知られている（1925–1965）》
- **male** 名 男, 雄

Word List

- **man-made** 形 人工の
- **manage** 動 ①動かす,うまく処理する ②経営[管理]する,支配する ③どうにか〜する
- **management** 名 ①経営,取り扱い ②運営,管理(側)
- **Manchuria** 名 満州《中国東北部,黒竜江省・吉林省・遼寧省にあたる地域の歴史的名称》
- **Manhattan** 名 マンハッタン
- **manifest** 形 表明する,明白な
- **manifest destiny** 《19世紀アメリカの》自明の宿命説《アメリカの移植者には,西部を開拓して領土を拡張する使命が与えられているとする,当時広く信じられた考え方》
- **Manila** 名 マニラ《フィリピンの首都》
- **Manuel Noriega** マヌエル・ノリエガ《パナマ共和国の軍人,政治家。1983年にパナマ軍最高司令官となって以降89年まで事実上の独裁者として君臨し,「ノリエガ将軍」の呼称で広く知られた(1934-2017)》
- **manufacturer** 名 製造業者,メーカー
- **manufacturing** 名 製造(業)
- **many** 熟 so many 非常に多くの
- **March on Washington for Jobs and Freedom** ワシントン大行進《1963年8月28日に,アメリカ合衆国のワシントンD.C.で行われた人種差別撤廃を求めるデモ》
- **mark** 動 ①印[記号]をつける ②目立たせる
- **market** 熟 stock market 株式市場
- **Marquis de La Fayette** ラファイエット《フランスの侯爵で,軍人,政治家。アメリカ独立革命とフランス革命の双方における活躍によって「両大陸の英雄」と讃えられた(1757-1834)》
- **Martin Luther King Jr.** マーティン・ルーサー・キング・ジュニア《アメリカ合衆国のプロテスタントバプテスト派の牧師。アフリカ系アメリカ人公民権運動の指導者として活動した(1929-1968)》
- **Martin Van Buren** マーティン・ヴァン・ビューレン《第8代アメリカ合衆国大統領(任期1837-1841)》
- **Maryland** 名 メリーランド州
- **Mason-Dixon line** メイソン＝ディクソン線《ペンシルベニア州,デラウェア州と,メリーランド州,ウェストバージニア州との間の州境の一部を定める境界線。一般に,アメリカ合衆国の北部と南部とを隔てる境界であると認識されている》
- **mass** 名 ①固まり,(密集した)集まり ②多数,多量 ③《the–es》大衆
- **Massachusetts** 名 マサチューセッツ州
- **Massachusetts Bay Colony** マサチューセッツ湾植民地《17世紀の北アメリカ東海岸にイギリスが創った植民地。ニューイングランドに属し,今日のセイラムとボストンを中心にしていた》
- **massacre** 名 大虐殺,皆殺し 動 虐殺する,殺りくする
- **massive** 形 ①巨大な,大量の ②堂々とした
- **match** 名 マッチ(棒)
- **material** 形 ①物質の,肉体的な ②不可欠な,重要な 名 材料,原料
  raw material 原料
- **matter of** 《a–》〜の問題
- **Mayflower** 名 メイフラワー号《ピルグリム・ファーザーズが1620年,イギリス南西部プリマスから,現在のアメリカ,マサチューセッツ州プリマスに渡ったときの船の名》
- **Mayflower Compact** メイフラワー誓約《メイフラワー号で北アメリカに渡ったピルグリム・ファーザーズが,プリマス植民地で作成し,のちのアメリカ連邦制の基礎の一つと

A Short History of America

なった文書。1620年11月20日, 乗船客100人以上のうち41人によって署名された》

- **McClellan** 名 ジョージ・マクレラン《アメリカ合衆国の軍人, 政治家。南北戦争中の, 北軍の少将(1826-1885)》
- **meaning** 名 ①意味, 趣旨 ②重要性
- **means of** ～する手段
- **meantime** 名 合間, その間 in the meantime それまでは, 当分は
- **meanwhile** 副 それまでの間, 一方では
- **measure** 名 ①寸法, 測定, 計量, 単位 ②程度, 基準 ③手段, 処置
- **Medellin drug cartel** メデジン・カルテル《コロンビアの犯罪組織。パブロ・エスコバルによりコロンビアのメデジンに創立された。麻薬密売者の組織化されたネットワーク》
- **media** 名 メディア, マスコミ, 媒体
- **Medicare** 名 メディケア《高齢者および障害者向け公的医療保険制度であり, 連邦政府が管轄している社会保険プログラム》
- **meeting** 名 集まり, ミーティング
- **memorable** 形 記憶すべき, 忘れられない
- **mention** 動 (～について)述べる, 言及する
- **mercenary** 名 (外国人の)雇い兵
- **merchant** 名 商人, 貿易商
- **method** 名 ①方法, 手段 ②秩序, 体系
- **Mexican** 形 メキシコ(人)の 名 メキシコ人
- **Mexican War** 米墨戦争《1846年から1848年の間にアメリカ合衆国とメキシコ合衆国(墨西哥)の間で戦われた戦争》
- **Mexico** 名 メキシコ《国名》
- **Mexico City** メキシコシティ《メキシコ合衆国の首都》
- **Michigan** 名 ミシガン州
- **Microsoft** 名 マイクロソフト《アメリカ合衆国ワシントン州に本社を置く, ソフトウェアを開発・販売する会社》
- **mid** 形 中央の, 中間の
- **mid-19th century** 19世紀半ば
- **middle** 名 中間, 最中 in the middle of ～の真ん中[真ほど]に 形 中間の, 中央の
- **Middle East** 中東
- **Midway** 名 ミッドウェー島《北太平洋のハワイ諸島北西にある環礁》
- **Midwestern** 形 アメリカ中西部の
- **might** 助《mayの過去》①～かもしれない ②～してもよい, ～できる
- **migrate** 動 移住する
- **migration** 名 移住, 移動
- **mile** 名 ①マイル《長さの単位。1,609m》②《-s》かなりの距離
- **military** 形 軍隊[軍人]の, 軍事の 名《the -》軍, 軍部
- **mine** 名 ①鉱山, 採鉱場
- **minister** 名 ①大臣, 閣僚, 公使 ②聖職者
- **Minnesota** 名 ミネソタ州
- **minority** 名 少数派, 少数民族
- **missile** 名 ミサイル
- **mission** 名 使命, 任務
- **Mississippi** 名 ミシシッピ州
- **Mississippi River** ミシシッピ川《北アメリカ大陸を流れる河川の1つ。ミネソタ州を源流とし, メキシコ湾へと注いでいる》
- **Missouri** 名 ミズーリ州
- **Missouri River** ミズーリ川《アメリカ合衆国中部を流れる川。ミシシッピ川の最も大きな支流》
- **Missouri Territory** ミズーリ準州
- **mob** 名 群集, やじ馬

- **model** 名 ①模型, 設計図 ②模範 ③(自動車などの)型, 様式
- **modern** 形 現代[近代]の, 現代的な, 最近の
- **Modern Republicanism** 近代的共和主義《ドワイト・D・アイゼンハワー大統領が推進した小さな政府, バランスの取れた予算, 政府支出の削減を軸とした保守的な財政政策》
- **moment** 名 ①瞬間, ちょっとの間 ②(特定の)時, 時期
- **monetary** 形 通貨の, 貨幣の, 金銭上の
- **money** 熟 make money お金を儲ける
- **monopoly** 名 独占, 専売(品)
- **Monroe Doctrine** モンロー主義《アメリカ合衆国がヨーロッパ諸国に対して, アメリカ大陸とヨーロッパ大陸間の相互不干渉を提唱したことを指す。第5代大統領ジェームズ・モンローが, 1823年に議会で行った7番目の年次教書演説で発表した》
- **morally** 副 道徳的に, 事実上
- **more** 熟 more and more ますます no more もう〜ない once more もう一度
- **Moscow** 名 モスクワ《ロシアの首都》
- **mosquito** 名 カ(蚊)
- **most** 熟 make the most of 〜を最大限利用する
- **mostly** 副 主として, 多くは, ほとんど
- **motion** 名 ①運動, 移動 ②身振り, 動作 motion picture 映画
- **motor** 名 ①モーター, 発動機 ②自動車《古》
- **movement** 名 ①動き, 運動 ②《-s》行動 ③引っ越し ④変動
- **Mulberry Street** マルベリー・ストリート《ニューヨークのイタリア街として栄えたリトル・イタリーのメインストリート。昔はマンハッタンで最悪のスラムの一つとされていたという》
- **mushroom** 名 ①キノコ, マッシュルーム ②キノコ状のもの mushroom cloud キノコ雲
- **musical** 名 ミュージカル
- **Mussolini** 名 ベニート・ムッソリーニ《イタリアの政治家, 教師, 軍人。国家ファシスト党による一党独裁制を確立した(1925–1943)》

N

- **nail** 名 ①爪 ②くぎ, びょう
- **name after** 〜にちなんで名付ける
- **Napoleon Bonaparte** ナポレオン・ボナパルト《革命期のフランスの軍人・政治家(1769–1821)》
- **Nat Turner** ナット・ターナー《アメリカ合衆国の奴隷であり, 奴隷反乱の指導者(1800–1831)》
- **Nathaniel Hawthorne** ナサニエル・ホーソーン《アメリカ合衆国の小説家(1804–1864)》
- **nation** 名 国, 国家,《the –》国民
- **national** 形 国家[国民]の, 全国の
- **National Labor Relations Board** 労働関係委員会
- **National Recovery Administration** 全国復興庁《全国産業復興法に基づき1933年に設立されたアメリカ合衆国の行政機関》
- **National Republican Party** 国民共和党《1824年から1833年までアメリカ合衆国に存在した, ジョン・クィンシー・アダムズの支持者と反ジャクソンを掲げる政治家の政党》
- **nationality** 名 国籍
- **nationwide** 副 全国的に
- **native** 形 ①出生(地)の, 自国の ②(〜に)固有の, 生まれつきの
- **Native American** ネイティブ・

A Short History of America

アメリカン《アメリカ合衆国の先住民族の総称》
- **naval** 形 海軍の
- **navigation** 名 航行, 航海, 操縦
- **navy** 名 海軍, 海軍力
- **Nazi (Party)** 国民社会主義ドイツ労働者党《1933年1月30日にヒトラーが首相に任命されたことで政権与党となり, 一党独裁体制を敷いたが, 1945年の第二次世界大戦の敗戦で事実上消滅し, 占領中に連合国によって禁止, 非合法化された》
- **nearly** 副 ①近くに, 親しく ②ほとんど, あやうく
- **Nebraska Territory** ネブラスカ準州
- **necessary** 形 必要な, 必然の
- **necessity** 名 必要, 不可欠, 必要品
- **negotiate** 動 交渉 [協議] する
- **negotiation** 名 交渉, 話し合い
- **Neil A. Armstrong** ニール・アームストロング《アメリカ合衆国の海軍飛行士, 宇宙飛行士。人類で初めて月面に降り立った。(1930-2012)》
- **neither** 形 どちらの〜も…でない 副《否定に続いて》〜も…しない neither 〜 nor … 〜も…もない
- **neo-industrial revolution** 新産業革命
- **neoconservative** 名 新保守主義《政治イデオロギーの1つで, 自由主義や民主主義を重視してアメリカの国益や実益よりも思想と理想を優先し, 武力介入も辞さない思想。略称ネオコン》
- **Netherlands** 名 オランダ《国名》
- **network** 名 回路, 網状組織, ネットワーク
- **neutral** 形 中立の, 中間的な
- **Nevada** 名 ネバダ州
- **New Amsterdam** ニューアムステルダム《オランダ植民地時代のニューヨークの名称》
- **New Deal** ニューディール政策《アメリカ合衆国大統領フランクリン・ルーズベルトが世界恐慌を克服するために行った一連の経済政策》
- **New England** ニューイングランド《アメリカ合衆国北東部の6州(北から南へメイン州, ニューハンプシャー州, バーモント州, マサチューセッツ州, ロードアイランド州, コネチカット州)を合わせた地方》
- **New England Confederation** ニューイングランド連合《清教徒革命前後のイギリス本国の混乱にともない, 政治的にも軍事的にも自立化を促されたニューイングランド諸植民地の連合》
- **New Frontier** ニューフロンティア《アメリカ合衆国第35代大統領のジョン・F・ケネディが打ち出した政策》
- **New Hampshire** ニューハンプシャー州
- **New Jersey** ニュージャージー州
- **New Mexico** ニューメキシコ州
- **New Orleans** ニューオーリンズ (ルイジアナ州)《都市名》
- **New World** アメリカ大陸, 新世界
- **New York** ニューヨーク《米国の都市;州》
- **New York City** ニューヨーク市
- **newly** 副 再び, 最近, 新たに
- **news** 名 報道, ニュース, 便り, 知らせ
- **Nikita Khrushchev** ニキータ・フルシチョフ《ソビエト連邦第4代最高指導者(在任1953-1964)》
- **Nimitz** 名 チェスター・ニミッツ《アメリカ海軍の軍人(1885-1966)》
- **Nineteenth Amendment** アメリカ合衆国憲法修正第19条《アメリカ合衆国の各州ならびに連邦政府が市民の性別を理由に市民の投票権を否定することを禁じたもの》

Word List

- **no longer** もはや~でない[~しない]
- **no more** もう~ない
- **nominate** 動 ①指名する,推薦する ②指定する
- **non-Anglican** 名 非英国教会系
- **non-white** 形 非白人の
- **none** 代 (~の)何も[誰も・少しも]…ない
- **nor** 接 ~もまたない　neither ~ nor … ~も…もない
- **normally** 副 普通は,通常は
- **Normandy** 名 《Invasion of –》ノルマンディー上陸作戦《第二次世界大戦中の1944年6月6日に連合軍によって行われたドイツ占領下の北西ヨーロッパへの侵攻作戦》
- **North America** 北アメリカ
- **North Korea** 朝鮮民主主義人民共和国
- **North Vietnam** ベトナム民主共和国《別称北ベトナム。1976年に南ベトナムを吸収併合したことで,ベトナム社会主義共和国として発展的に消滅》
- **northeastern** 形 北東の
- **northern** 形 北の,北向きの,北からの
- **northwest** 名 北西(部)
- **not ~ but …** ~ではなくて…
- **not always** 必ずしも~であるとは限らない
- **not only ~ but (also) …** ~だけでなく…もまた
- **not yet** まだ~してない
- **note** 動 ①書き留める ②注意[注目]する
- **novel** 名 (長編)小説
- **now that** 今や~だから、~からには
- **nuclear** 形 核の,原子力の
- **Nuclear Test Ban Treaty** 部分的核実験禁止条約《1963年8月5日にアメリカ,イギリス,ソ連との間で調印された,核兵器の一部の実験を禁止する条約》
- **Nueces River** ヌエイシス川《メキシコ湾へと流れるテキサス州の川》
- **number of** 《a –》いくつかの~,多くの~
- **nursing** 名 看病,育児

O

- **Oberlin** 名 オーバリン大学《オハイオ州オーバリンに本部を置くアメリカ合衆国のリベラル・アーツ・カレッジ大学。1833年設置》
- **occupy** 動 ①占領する,保有する ②居住する ③占める ④(職に)つく,従事する
- **occur** 動 (事が)起こる,生じる,(考えなどが)浮かぶ
- **of course** もちろん,当然
- **offer** 動 申し出る,申し込む,提供する
- **officer** 名 役人,公務員,警察官
- **officially** 副 公式に,職務上,正式に
- **Ohio** 名 オハイオ州
- **oil** 名 油,石油
- **Old Ironsides** オールド・アイアンサイズ《アメリカ海軍の木造船殻,3本マスト,砲数44門のフリゲート,USSコンスティチューションの愛称》
- **Omnibus Bill of 1850** 1850年協定《米墨戦争から発生した領地と奴隷制の議論で決められた一連の法律。5つの法律が南部の奴隷所有州と,自由州の利益のバランスを取った》
- **once more** もう一度
- **one side** 片側
- **one-third** 3分の1
- **only** 熟 not only ~ but (also) …

〜だけでなく…もまた
- **operation** 名 ①操作, 作業, 動作 ②経営, 運営 ③手術 ④作戦, 軍事行動 come into operation 動き始める, 作動し始める
- **opponent** 名 競争相手, 敵, 反対者
- **opportunity** 名 好機, 適当な時期［状況］
- **oppose** 動 反対する, 敵対する
- **opposition** 名 ①反対 ②野党
- **oppression** 名 圧迫, 抑圧, 重荷
- **order** 熟 in order to 〜するために, 〜しようと
- **ordinary** 形 ①普通の, 通常の ②並の, 平凡な
- **Oregon** 名 オレゴン州
- **Oregon Territory** オレゴン準州
- **Oregon Trail** オレゴン・トレイル《19世紀, 北アメリカ大陸の西部開拓時代にアメリカ合衆国の開拓者達が通った主要道の一つ》
- **organization** 名 ①組織(化), 編成, 団体, 機関 ②有機体, 生物
- **organize** 動 組織する
- **originally** 副 ①元は, 元来 ②独創的に
- **other** 熟 each other お互いに in other words すなわち, 言い換えれば on the other hand 一方, 他方では
- **Ottoman Empire** オスマン帝国《小アジアを中心に北アフリカ, 西アジア, バルカン, 黒海北部, カフカス南部を支配したイスラム帝国。1299年から1922年まで存続》
- **out of** 〜から外へ, 〜を超越して
- **outcome** 名 結果, 結末
- **outlawing** 名 違法化
- **outrage** 名 暴力, 暴行, 乱暴
- **outskirt** 名 はずれ《都市または町の中心から遠く離れた所》
- **overinvestment** 名 過剰投資
- **overseas** 副 海外へ
- **owner** 名 持ち主, オーナー

P

- **pacific** 形《P-》太平洋の 名《the P-》太平洋
- **Pacific Ocean** 太平洋
- **paid** 形 有給の, 支払い済みのの
- **Palestine** 名 パレスチナ
- **pamphlet** 名 パンフレット, 小冊子
- **Pan-American Exposition** パン・アメリカン博覧会《1901年にニューヨーク州バッファローで開催》
- **Panama** 名 パナマ共和国
- **Panama Canal** パナマ運河《パナマ共和国のパナマ地峡を開削して太平洋とカリブ海を結んでいる閘門式運河》
- **panic** 名 パニック, 恐慌
- **Panic of 1837** 1837年恐慌《1840年代まで続いた大きな景気後退を誘発したアメリカ合衆国の金融危機》
- **Panic of 1907** 1907年恐慌《アメリカ合衆国で1907年10月に発生した金融恐慌》
- **parallel** 名 平行線 38th parallel 北緯38度線《第二次世界大戦末期に朝鮮半島を横切る北緯38度線に引かれたアメリカ軍とソ連軍の分割占領ライン》
- **Paris** 名 パリ《フランスの首都》
- **parliament** 名 国会, 議会
- **part** take part in 〜に参加する
- **participate** 動 参加する, 加わる
- **particularly** 副 特に, とりわけ
- **partly** 副 一部分は, ある程度は
- **passage** 名 ①通過, 通行, 通路 ②一節, 経過

WORD LIST

- **passenger** 名 乗客, 旅客
- **passion** 名 情熱, (～への)熱中, 激怒
- **passionate** 形 情熱的な, (感情が)激しい, 短気な
- **path** 名 ①(踏まれてできた)小道, 歩道 ②進路, 通路
- **Patrick Henry** パトリック・ヘンリー《アメリカの政治家。1775年3月23日, イギリスの支配に異議を唱えるニューイングランド地方の抵抗運動へのバージニアの参加を訴えた演説における「自由を与えよ。然らずんば死を」という発言は歴史に記憶される名文句 (1736–1799)》
- **Patriots' Day** パトリオット・デイ《愛国者の日。マサチューセッツ州, メイン州, ウィスコンシン州の3州において制定されている祝日。アメリカ独立戦争の緒戦となる1775年4月19日のレキシントン・コンコードの戦いを記念したもの。4月の第3月曜日》
- **patronage system** 猟官制《公職の任命を政治的背景に基づいて行うこと。選挙で政権政党が交替するたびに中央・地方を問わず公務員のほとんどが新しい政権政党の人物に変更される》
- **pay** 動 ①支払う, 払う, 報いる, 償う ②割に合う, ペイする **pay back** 返済する
- **peacefully** 副 平和に, 穏やかに
- **Pearl Harbor** 真珠湾《アメリカ合衆国ハワイ州オアフ島にある入り江の一つであり, 湾内にはアメリカ海軍の軍事拠点(軍港)などが置かれている》
- **peninsula** 名 半島
- **Pennsylvania** ペンシルベニア州
- **Pentagon** 名 ペンタゴン, 米国国防総省(の建物)
- **People's Republic of China** 中華人民共和国
- **perhaps** 副 たぶん, ことによると
- **period** 名 ①期, 期間, 時代 ②ピリオド, 終わり
- **perish** 動 滅びる, 死ぬ
- **permanent** 形 永続する, 永久の, 長持ちする
- **persecution** 名 迫害, 虐待
- **persistent** 形 ①しつこい, 頑固な ②持続する, 永続的な
- **persuade** 動 説得する, 促して～させる
- **Peter Zenger** ジョン・ピーター・ゼンガー《イギリス支配下のニューヨーク植民地で印刷業者, 出版業者として活動したドイツ系アメリカ植民地人 (1697–1746)》
- **Philadelphia** 名 フィラデルフィア(ペンシルベニア州)《都市名》
- **Philippine–American War** 米比戦争《アメリカ合衆国とフィリピンの間で1899年–1902年に起きた戦争》
- **Philippines** 名 フィリピン《国名》
- **philosophy** 名 哲学, 主義, 信条, 人生観
- **phonograph** 名 蓄音機
- **phrase** 名 句, 慣用句, 名言
- **pick up** 再開する, 回復する
- **Pilgrims** 名 ピルグリム・ファーザーズ《1620年, メイフラワー号で北アメリカに移住したイギリス人入植者で, 最初の入植地となったプリマス植民地を築いた人々》
- **pioneer** 名 開拓者, 先駆者
- **pipe** 名 管, パイプ
- **place** 熟 **put in place** ～を整備する **take place** 行われる, 起こる
- **placer** 名 砂鉱 **placer deposit** 砂鉱床
- **plantation** 名 大農園, 植林地
- **player** 名 ①競技者, 選手, 演奏者, 俳優 ②演奏装置
- **plow** 名 鋤, プラウ《農具》

A Short History of America

- **Plymouth** 名 プリマス（デヴォン州）《都市名》
- **point of view** 考え方, 視点
- **point out** 指し示す, 指摘する, 目を向ける, 目を向けさせる
- **policy** 名 ①政策, 方針, 手段 ②保険証券
- **Polish-Lithuanian Commonwealth** ポーランド・リトアニア共和国（1569-1795）
- **political** 形 ①政治の, 政党の ②策略的な political struggle 政治闘争
- **politician** 名 政治家, 政略家
- **politics** 名 政治（学）, 政策
- **pool** 名 水たまり, プール
- **poorly** 副 ①貧しく, 乏しく ②ヘたに
- **popularity** 名 人気, 流行
- **population** 名 人口, 住民（数）
- **pork** 名 豚肉
- **port** 名 港, 港町, 空港
- **portrait** 名 肖像画
- **Portuguese** 形 ポルトガル（人・語）の 名 ①ポルトガル人 ②ポルトガル語
- **position** 名 ①位置, 場所, 姿勢 ②地位, 身分, 職 ③立場, 状況
- **possession** 名 ①所有（物）②財産, 領土
- **possible** 形 ①可能な ②ありうる, 起こりうる as ~ as possible できるだけ~
- **postal** 形 郵便の, 郵送の
- **poster** 名 ポスター
- **postwar** 形 戦後の
- **Potomac River** ポトマック川《アメリカ合衆国の中部大西洋沿岸のチェサピーク湾の中へ流れ込む河川》
- **Potsdam Declaration** ポツダム宣言《1945年7月26日にアメリカ合衆国大統領, イギリス首相, 中華民国主席の名において大日本帝国に対して発された,「全日本軍の無条件降伏」等を求めた宣言》
- **powerful** 形 力強い, 実力のある, 影響力のある
- **powerless** 形 力のない, 頼りない, 弱い
- **practical** 形 ①実際的な, 実用的な, 役に立つ ②経験を積んだ
- **prefer** 動（~のほうを）好む,（~のほうが）よいと思う
- **prejudice** 名 偏見, 先入観
- **prepare for** ~の準備をする
- **presence** 名 ①存在すること ②出席, 態度
- **preservation** 名 保護, 保守
- **presidency** 名 大統領の任務[任期]
- **president** 名 ①大統領 ②社長, 学長, 頭取
- **presidential** 形 大統領の
- **press** 動 ①圧する, 押す, プレスする ②強要する, 迫る 名 ①圧迫, 押し, 切迫 ②出版物［社］, 新聞 freedom of the press 出版［報道・言論］の自由
- **prevent** 動 ①妨げる, じゃまする ②予防する, 守る,《-~ from …》~が…できない［しない］ようにする
- **price** 名 ①値段, 代価 ②《-s》物価, 相場
- **priest** 名 聖職者, 牧師, 僧侶
- **primary** 形 第一の, 主要な, 最初の, 初期の
- **Princeton** 名 プリンストン（ニュージャージー州）《地名》
- **principle** 名 ①原理, 原則 ②道義, 正道
- **printer** 名 ①印刷機, プリンター ②印刷業者
- **printing** 名 印刷, 焼き付け printing press 印刷機

Word List

- **prison** 名 ①刑務所, 監獄 ②監禁
- **private** 形 ①私的な, 個人の ②民間の, 私立の ③内密の, 人里離れた
- **pro-U.S.** 形 親米の
- **proactive** 形 (行動などが)先を見越した, 先回りした, 積極的な
- **probably** 副 たぶん, あるいは
- **process** 名 ①過程, 経過, 進行 ②手順, 方法, 製法, 加工
- **proclamation** 名 宣言, 声明
- **product** 名 ①製品, 産物 ②成果, 結果
- **production** 名 製造, 生産
- **productive** 形 生産的な, 豊富な
- **profitably** 副 有利に, もうけになるように
- **progress** 名 ①進歩, 前進 ②成り行き, 経過 make progress 進歩[上達]する, 前進する
- **progressive** 形 進歩的な, 前進する
- **prohibit** 動 ①禁止する, 差し止める ②妨げる, 予防する
- **prohibition** 名 禁止, 差し止め
- **Prohibition** 名 禁酒法《アメリカ合衆国憲法修正第18条により1920年から施行された酒類の製造・販売などを禁止した制度(1933年の憲法修正により廃止)》
- **project** 名 計画, プロジェクト
- **prominent** 形 ①突き出た ②傑出した, 目立つ
- **promote** 動 促進する, 昇進[昇級]させる
- **property** 名 ①財産, 所有物[地] ②性質, 属性
- **propose** 動 ①申し込む, 提案する ②結婚を申し込む
- **prosper** 動 栄える, 繁栄する, 成功する
- **prosperity** 名 繁栄, 繁盛, 成功
- **protection** 名 保護, 保護するもの[人]
- **protest** 動 ①主張[断言]する ②抗議する, 反対する 名 抗議(書), 不服
- **Protestant** 名 プロテスタント 形 プロテスタントの
- **Protestantism** 名 プロテスタント主義
- **provide** 動 ①供給する, 用意する, (~に)備える ②規定する
- **public** 形 公の, 公開の
- **publication** 名 ①出版(物) ②公表, 広報
- **publish** 動 ①発表[公表]する ②出版[発行]する
- **publisher** 名 出版社, 発行者
- **Puerto Rico** プエルトリコ
- **pumpkin** 名 カボチャ
- **punish** 動 罰する, ひどい目にあわせる
- **purchase** 動 購入する, 獲得する 名 購入(物), 仕入れ, 獲得
- **Puritan** 名 ピューリタン, 清教徒《イングランド国教会の改革を唱えたキリスト教のプロテスタント(カルヴァン派)の大きなグループ》
- **pursue** 動 ①追う, つきまとう ②追求する, 従事する
- **pursuit** 名 追跡, 追求
- **push back** 押し返す, 押しのける
- **put in** ~の中に入れる
- **put in place** ~を整備する
- **put ~ into ...** ~を…の状態にする put ~ into effect (法律など)の発効を命ずる
- **puzzle** 動 迷わせる, 当惑する[させる]

Q

- **Quaker** 名 クエーカー《キリスト教

プロテスタントの一派であるキリスト友会に対する一般的な呼称》
- **qualify** 動 ①資格を得る[与える] ②《文法で》修飾する
- **quality** 名 ①質, 性質, 品質 ②特性 ③良質
- **Quebec** 名 ケベック州(カナダ)
- **Quebec, battle of** ケベックの戦い《アメリカ独立戦争初期の大陸軍によるカナダ侵攻作戦中, 1775年12月31日にケベック市を守るイギリス軍との間に行われた戦闘》
- **Queenston Heights, battle of** クィーンストン・ハイツの戦い《米英戦争の初期である1812年10月13日に, 現在のオンタリオ州クィーンストン近くでイギリス軍とアメリカ軍との間に戦われた戦闘》
- **quickly** 副 敏速に, 急いで

R

- **racism** 名 人種差別, 人種差別主義
- **radical** 形 急進的な, 過激な
- **radically** 副 急進的に, 過激に
- **railroad** 名 鉄道, 路線
- **Ralph Waldo Emerson** ラルフ・ワルド・エマーソン《アメリカ合衆国の思想家, 哲学者, 作家, 詩人(1803–1882)》
- **rate** 名 割合, 率
- **rather** 副 ①むしろ, かえって ②かなり, いくぶん, やや ③それどころか逆に rather than 〜よりむしろ
- **ratify** 動 承認する, 批准する
- **raw** 形 ①生の, 未加工の ②未熟な raw material 原料
- **re-elect** 動 〜を再選する
- **reaction** 名 反応, 反動, 反抗, 影響
- **ready to** すぐに[いつでも]〜できる, 〜する構えで
- **real estate** 不動産, 土地
- **reality** 名 現実, 実在, 真実(性)
- **realize** 動 理解する, 実現する
- **rebel** 名 反逆者, 反抗者, 謀反人 動 反抗する, 反逆する
- **recent** 形 近ごろの, 近代の
- **recently** 副 近ごろ, 最近
- **recession** 名 景気後退, 不況, 後退
- **reconciliation** 名 和解, 仲直り, 調停
- **reconsider** 動 考え直す, 再検討する
- **reconstruct** 動 再建する, 再現する
- **reconstruction** 名 再建, 復興, 復元
- **Reconstruction** 名 レコンストラクション《アメリカ南北戦争によりアメリカ連合国と奴隷制システムが崩壊した後の問題を解決しようとする, 1863年(または1865年)から1877年までの過程を意味するアメリカ合衆国史の用語》
- **Reconstruction Act** 再建法《アメリカ南北戦争後, 南部の再建と連邦への復帰の条件を規定した諸法律。1867年3月2日, 連邦議会がアンドリュー・ジョンソン大統領の拒否権を乗り越えて制定した》
- **recover** 動 ①取り戻す, ばん回する ②回復する
- **recovery** 名 回復, 復旧, 立ち直り
- **recruit** 動 (人材を)募集する, 勧誘する
- **reduce** 動 ①減じる ②しいて〜させる, (〜の)状態にする
- **reduction** 名 ①下げること, 減少, 値下げ, 割引 ②縮図 ③換算, 約分, 還元
- **reform** 動 改善する, 改革する 名 改善, 改良
- **refuse** 動 拒絶する, 断る
- **region** 名 ①地方, 地域 ②範囲
- **regulation** 名 規則, 規定, 規制

Word List

- **relate** 動 ①関連がある, かかわる, うまく折り合う ②物語る
- **relation** 名 ①(利害)関係, 間柄 ②親族
- **relationship** 名 関係, 関連, 血縁関係
- **religion** 名 宗教, ~教, 信条
- **religious** 形 ①宗教の ②信心深い
- **remain** 動 ①残っている, 残る ②(~の)ままである[いる]
- **removal** 名 除去, 移動
- **remove** 動 ①取り去る, 除去する ②(衣類を)脱ぐ
- **Renaissance** 名 ①《the -》ルネッサンス, 文芸復興(運動) ②ルネッサンス様式 ③《時にr-》(芸術・学問の)復興
- **reorganize** 動 再編成する, 再組織する
- **reply** 動 答える, 返事をする, 応答する
- **represent** 動 ①表現する ②意味する ③代表する
- **representation** 名 表現, 代表, 代理
- **representative** 名 ①代表(者), 代理人 ②代議士
- **republic** 名 共和国
- **Republic of Texas** テキサス共和国《現在の米国テキサス州およびその周囲の地域が分離, 独立して短期間存在した共和国(1836-1845)》
- **republican** 形 共和国の, 共和主義の, 共和党の 名 共和主義者, 共和党員
- **Republican Party** 共和党
- **republicanism** 名 共和主義《政治思想の一つ。共和国・共和制といった政体の構成原理》
- **require** 動 ①必要とする, 要する ②命じる, 請求する
- **resentment** 名 怒り, 立腹, うらみ
- **reservation** 名 ①留保, 制限 ②予約, 指定
- **reserve** 動 とっておく, 備えておく 名 ①蓄え, 備え ②準備[積立]金
- **resign** 動 辞職する, やめる, 断念する
- **resignation** 名 ①辞任, 辞表 ②あきらめ
- **resist** 動 抵抗[反抗・反撃]する, 耐える
- **resistance** 名 抵抗, 反抗, 敵対
- **resource** 名 ①資源, 財産 ②手段, 方策
- **respect** 動 尊敬[尊重]する
- **respond** 動 答える, 返答[応答]する
- **responsible** 形 責任のある, 信頼できる, 確実な
- **restore** 動 元に戻す, 復活させる
- **restraint** 名 ①自制, 抑制 ②拘束
- **restrict** 動 制限する, 禁止する
- **result** 名 結果, 成り行き, 成績 as a result その結果(として) as a result of ~の結果(として) 動 (結果として)起こる, 生じる, 結局~になる
- **retire** 動 引き下がる, 退職[引退]する
- **retreat** 動 後退する, 退く
- **return** 熟 in return for ~に対する見返りとして, ~の交換条件として return to ~に戻る, ~に帰る
- **reunite** 動 再結合する
- **revival** 名 復活, 再生, リバイバル
- **revive** 動 生き返る, 生き返らせる, 復活する[させる]
- **revolt** 動 そむく, 反乱を起こす
- **revolution** 名 ①革命, 変革 ②回転, 旋回
- **revolutionary** 形 革命の, 画期的な, 革命的な
- **Revolutionary War** アメリカ

A SHORT HISTORY OF AMERICA

独立戦争《1775年4月19日から1783年9月3日までの, イギリス本国とアメリカ東部沿岸のイギリス領の13植民地との戦争》

- **revolutionist** 名 革命家
- **Rhode Island** ロードアイランド州
- **Richard M. Nixon** リチャード・ニクソン《第37代アメリカ合衆国大統領(任期1969-1974)》
- **Richard Warren Sears** リチャード・ウォーレン・シアーズ《小売業の新時代を築いた シアーズの創業者。カタログを郵送して, 一括仕入れで安価に商品を提供するダイレクト・マーケティングを推し進めた(1863-1914)》
- **Richmond** 名 リッチモンド(バージニア州)《都市名》
- **rider** 名(自転車・オートバイ・馬などの)乗り手, ライダー
- **right** 熟 all right 大丈夫で, よろしい, 申し分ない right away すぐに
- **Rio Grande River** リオ・グランデ川《アメリカ合衆国のコロラド州から流れ出しメキシコ湾へ注ぐ川》
- **riot** 名 暴動, 騒動
- **rise** 熟 give rise to ~を引き起こす
- **risk** 動 危険にさらす, 賭ける, 危険をおかす
- **ritual** 名 ①儀式 ②行事 ③慣例
- **rival** 名 競争相手, 匹敵する人
- **roam** 動 ぶらぶら歩き回る, 放浪する
- **Robert de La Salle** ロベール゠カブリエ・ド・ラ・サール《フランス人探検家。ミシシッピベイスン全体をフランス領として主張し, 「ルイジアナ」と名付けた人物(1643-1687)》
- **Robert E. Lee** ロバート・E・リー《南北戦争の時代のアメリカの軍人。南部連合の軍司令官を務め, 北軍を大いに苦しめた(1807-1870)》
- **Robert Fulton** ロバート・フルトン《アメリカ合衆国の技術者で発明家。ハドソン川で蒸気船の実験と実用化に成功した(1765-1815)》
- **Roger Williams** ロジャー・ウィリアムズ《イギリス生まれの神学者(1603-1683)》
- **role** 名 ①(劇などの)役 ②役割, 任務
- **Ronald W. Reagan** ロナルド・レーガン《第40代アメリカ合衆国大統領(任期1981-1989)》
- **rough** 形 ①(手触りが)粗い ②荒々しい, 未加工の
- **Rough Riders** 第1合衆国義勇騎兵隊《1898年に編成されたアメリカ陸軍の義勇騎兵隊連隊。通称ラフ・ライダーズ》
- **route** 名 道, 道筋, 進路, 回路
- **ruin** 名 破滅, 滅亡, 破産, 廃墟
- **rumor** 名 うわさ
- **runaway** 形 逃げた, 手に負えない
- **rural** 形 田舎の, 地方の
- **rush** 動 突進する, せき立てる
- **Russia** 名 ロシア《国名》
- **Russian** 名 ロシア(人・語)の 名 ①ロシア人 ②ロシア語
- **Russian Empire** ロシア帝国《1721年から1917年までに存在した帝国》
- **Rutherford B. Hayes** ラザフォード・ヘイズ《第19代アメリカ合衆国大統領(任期1877-1881)》

S

- **Saddam Hussein** サダム・フセイン《イラク共和国の政治家(1937-2006)》
- **sadly** 副 悲しそうに, 不幸にも
- **safety** 名 安全, 無事, 確実
- **sail** 名 ①帆, 帆船 ②帆走, 航海 set sail 出帆[出航]する 動 帆走する, 航

Word List

海する, 出航する
- **sailing ship** 帆船
- **sailor** 名 船員, (ヨットの)乗組員
- **Saint Lawrence River** セントローレンス川《北米大陸の五大湖と大西洋を結んでカナダ東部を東北に流れる河川》
- **SALT II** 第二次戦略兵器制限交渉《Strategic Arms Limitation Talks II の略称。1979年6月18日, アメリカ合衆国とソビエト連邦との間で行われた, 互いの核兵器の数を制限する交渉, およびその結果締結された軍備制限条約》
- **salty** 形 塩の, 塩を含む
- **same** 熟 at the same time as 〜 と同時に
- **Samuel Adams** サミュエル・アダムズ《アメリカ合衆国の指導者, 政治家, 著作家, 政治哲学者であり, アメリカ合衆国建国の父の一人 (1722-1803)》
- **Samuel Houston** サミュエル・ヒューストン《19世紀のアメリカ合衆国の軍人, 政治家。テネシー州とテキサス州という二つの異なった州で知事を務めた (1793-1863)》
- **Samuel J. Tilden** サミュエル・ティルデン《アメリカ合衆国の弁護士, 政治家。1876年大統領選挙に民主党候補として出馬したが, 選挙人投票でわずか1票差で敗れた (1814-1886)》
- **sank** 動 sink (沈む)の過去
- **Santa Anna** アントニオ・ロペス・デ・サンタ・アナ《メキシコの軍人, 政治家。1833年から1855年までの間に11回も大統領に選ばれた (1794-1876)》
- **Saratoga** サラトガ (ニューヨーク州)《町名》
- **satellite** 名 ①(人工)衛星 ②衛星国, 取り巻き
- **savage** 形 どう猛な, 残忍な
- **scale** 名 規模, 割合, 程度, スケール
- **scandal** 名 スキャンダル, 醜聞

- **scatter** 動 ①ばらまく, 分散する ②《be -ed》散在する
- **schooling** 名 学校教育, 教室授業, スクーリング
- **search** 名 捜査, 探索, 調査 in search of 〜を探し求めて
- **Second Continental Congress** 第2次大陸会議《1775年5月10日から1781年3月1日まで, 開催されたアメリカ13植民地の代表による会議》
- **Second National Bank of the United States** 第二合衆国銀行《1817年1月にアメリカ合衆国議会によって公認されたアメリカ合衆国の銀行》
- **Second World War** 第二次世界大戦《1939年から1945年までの6年間, ドイツ, 日本, イタリアの日独伊三国同盟を中心とする枢軸国陣営と, イギリス, ソビエト連邦, アメリカ, 中華民国などの連合国陣営との間で戦われた全世界的規模の巨大戦争》
- **secret** 形 ①秘密の, 隠れた ②神秘の, 不思議な
- **Secretariat** 名 事務局
- **secretary** 名 ①秘書, 書記 ②《S-》長官, 大臣
- **Secretary of State** アメリカ合衆国国務長官《アメリカ合衆国の外交を担当する閣僚》
- **Secretary of the Treasury** アメリカ合衆国財務長官《アメリカ合衆国財務省の長官であり, 連邦政府において金融政策および財政政策を担当する閣僚》
- **secretly** 副 秘密に, 内緒で
- **sector** 名 (産業などの)部門, セクター
- **security** 名 ①安全(性), 安心 ②担保, 抵当, 《-ties》有価証券
- **Security Council** 国際連合安全保障理事会《国際連合の主要機関の一つ。事実上の最高意思決定機関》

A Short History of America

- see ~ as ... ~を…と考える
- see if ~かどうかを確かめる
- seek 動 捜し求める, 求める
- seem 動 (~に)見える, (~のように)思われる
- seen as 熟《be -》~として見られる
- segregate 動 分離する, 隔離する
- seize 動 ①ぐっとつかむ, 捕らえる ②襲う
- select 動 選択する, 選ぶ
- selection 名 選択(物), 選抜, 抜粋
- senator 名 上院議員, 元老院議員, (大学の)評議員
- sense 名 ①感覚, 感じ ②《-s》意識, 正気, 本性 ③常識, 分別, センス ④意味
- separated 形 分かれた, 別れた, 別々の
- separation 名 分離(点), 離脱, 分類, 別離
- series 名 一続き, 連続, シリーズ
- serious 形 ①まじめな, 真剣な ②重大な, 深刻な, (病気などが)重い
- serve 動 ①仕える, 奉仕する ②(役目を)果たす, 務める, 役に立つ
- service 名 ①勤務, 業務 ②公益事業 ③点検, 修理 ④奉仕, 貢献 civil service (軍・司法・立法関係以外)政府官吏, (軍関係以外の)文官, 公務員
- session 名 ①授業(期間) ②会期, 開会 ③講座, 集まり
- set sail 出帆[出航]する
- set up 配置する, セットする, 据え付ける, 設置する
- settle 動 ①安定する[させる], 落ち着く, 落ち着かせる ②《- in ~》~に移り住む, 定住する
- settlement 名 ①定住, 入植地, 集落 ②合意, 解決, 清算
- settler 名 移住者, 入植者
- Seven Years War 七年戦争《プロイセン王国とオーストリアの対立を軸に, プロイセンはイギリス, オーストリアはフランス, ロシアと結び, 全ヨーロッパに広がった戦争 (1756-1763)》
- severe 形 厳しい, 深刻な, 激しい
- severely 副 厳しく, 簡素に
- sex 名 性, 性別, 男女
- shaken 動 shake(振る)の過去分詞
- shelter 名 ①避難所, 隠れ家 ②保護, 避難
- Sherman Anti-Trust Act of 1890 シャーマン法《1890年に制定された米国の連邦法で, 反トラスト法の中心的な法律のひとつ》
- shook 動 shake(振る)の過去
- shortage 名 不足, 欠乏
- shortly 副 まもなく, すぐに
- shown 動 show(見せる)の過去分詞
- side 名 側, 横, そば, 斜面 one side 片側
- significant 形 ①重要な, 有意義な ②大幅な, 著しい ③意味ありげな
- silhouette 名 シルエット, 影絵, 輪郭
- silver 名 銀, 銀貨, 銀色 形 銀製の
- similar 形 同じような, 類似した, 相似の be similar to ~に似ている
- singer 名 歌手, シンガー
- single 形 ①たった1つの ②1人用の, それぞれの
- situation 名 ①場所, 位置 ②状況, 境遇, 立場
- slave 名 奴隷
- slavery 名 奴隷制度, 奴隷状態
- slogan 名 スローガン, モットー
- slowly 副 遅く, ゆっくり
- smoking 名 喫煙 形 煙っている, 喫煙の

WORD LIST

- **smuggling** 名密輸
- **so** 熟 and so on 〜など、その他もろもろ so many 非常に多くの so that 〜するために、それで、〜できるように so 〜 that … 非常に〜なので…
- **so-called** 形 いわゆる
- **social** 形 ①社会の、社会的な ②社交的な、愛想のよい
- **socialism** 名 社会主義(運動)
- **socially** 副 社交的に、社交上
- **society** 名 社会、世間
- **Society of Jesus** イエズス会《キリスト教、カトリック教会の男子修道会》
- **soil** 名 土、土地
- **soldier** 名 兵士、兵卒
- **solo** 形 単独の
- **Solomon Islands** ソロモン諸島《南太平洋のメラネシアにある島嶼群であり、またその島々を国土とする国家》
- **solution** 名 ①分解、溶解 ②解決、解明、回答
- **solve** 動 解く、解決する
- **someone** 代 ある人、誰か
- **sometimes** 副 時々、時たま
- **Sons of Liberty** 自由の息子達《アメリカ独立戦争以前における北米13植民地の愛国急進派の通称。サミュエル・アダムズが中心となったボストンの組織は、1773年にボストン茶会事件を引き起こした》
- **soon** 熟 as soon as 〜するとすぐ、〜するや否や
- **sort** 動 分類する sort out 〜を整理[解決]する
- **sought** 動 seek (捜し求める)の過去、過去分詞
- **source** 名 源、原因、もと
- **South Carolina** サウスカロライナ州
- **South Korea** 大韓民国
- **South Vietnam** ベトナム共和国《1955年から1975年までベトナム南部に存在した国家。略称南ベトナム》
- **southeast** 名 南東(部) 形 南東の、南東向きの
- **southeastern** 形 南東(地方)の、南東への
- **Southeast(ern) Asia** 東南アジア
- **southern** 形 南の、南向きの、南からの
- **Southern Confederate** アメリカ連合国《かつて北アメリカに存在した国家。アメリカ合衆国から分離して独立を宣言した南部諸州によって1861年に創設。南北戦争の敗北により1865年に消滅した》
- **southwestern** 名 南西(部) 形 南西の、南西向きの
- **Soviet Union** ソビエト連邦《1922年から1991年までの間に存在したユーラシア大陸における共和制国家》
- **Spain** 名 スペイン《国名》
- **Spanish** 形 スペイン(人・語)の 名 ①スペイン人 ②スペイン語
- **Spanish Armada** スペイン無敵艦隊《1588年スペイン王フェリペ2世がイギリス制圧のために派遣した艦隊。ドーバー海峡でイギリス艦隊に大敗。以後スペインの制海権は失われた》
- **Spanish–American War** 米西戦争《1898年にアメリカ合衆国とスペインの間で起きた戦争》
- **speak of** 〜を口にする
- **spending** 名 支出、出費
- **Spirit of St. Louis** スピリットオブセントルイス号《チャールズ・リンドバーグによって、ノンストップ大西洋横断単独飛行に成功した単発機の愛称》
- **spoil** 動 ①台なしにする、だめにな

る ②甘やかす
- **spoils system** 猟官制《公職の任命を政治的背景に基づいて行うこと。選挙で政権政党が交替するたびに中央・地方を問わず公務員のほとんどが新しい政権政党系の人物に変更される》
- **Sputnik I** スプートニク1号《ソビエト連邦が1957年10月4日に打ち上げた世界初の人工衛星》
- **Sputnik II** スプートニク2号《ソビエト連邦が1957年11月3日に打ち上げた人工衛星・宇宙船。イヌを乗せており、世界初の宇宙船となったもの》
- **squash** 名 カボチャ
- **stability** 名 安定(性)、持続
- **stable** 形 安定した、堅固な、分解しにくい
- **stamp** 名 ①印 ②切手
- **Stamp Act of 1765** 印紙法《1765年3月にイギリスがアメリカ植民地に対して課した印紙税を定めた法》
- **stand up against** 〜に抵抗する
- **standard** 名 標準、規格、規準
- **state** 名 ①あり様、状態 ②国家、(アメリカなどの)州 ③階層、地位 動 述べる、表明する
- **statement** 名 声明、述べること
- **steamboat** 名 蒸気船
- **steel** 名 鋼、鋼鉄(製の物)
- **Stephen A. Douglas** スティーブン・ダグラス《アメリカ合衆国西部のイリノイ州出身の政治家。1860年の民主党大統領指名候補となるが、エイブラハム・リンカーンに敗れた(1813–1861)》
- **stock** 名 ①貯蔵 ②仕入れ品、在庫品 ③株式 **stock market** 株式市場
- **storm** 名 ①嵐、暴風雨 ②強襲
- **stove** 名 ①レンジ、こんろ ②ストーブ

- **strait** 名 海峡
- **strategic** 形 戦略的な、戦略上の
- **Strategic Arms Limitation Talks II** 第二次戦略兵器制限交渉《1979年6月18日、アメリカ合衆国とソビエト連邦との間で行われた、互いの核兵器の数を制限する交渉、およびその結果締結された軍備制限条約。略称SALT II》
- **strategy** 名 戦略、作戦、方針
- **strength** 名 ①力、体力 ②長所、強み ③強度、濃度
- **strengthen** 動 強くする、しっかりさせる
- **strict** 形 厳しい、厳密な
- **strictly** 副 厳しく、厳密に
- **strike** 名 ストライキ
- **strongly** 副 強く、頑丈に、猛烈に、熱心に
- **struggle** 動 もがく、奮闘する 名 ①もがき、奮闘 ②争い、闘争 **political struggle** 政治闘争
- **subject** 名 (国王などの)臣民、臣下
- **submarine** 名 潜水艦
- **substantial** 形 実体の、本質的な、実質上の
- **succeed** 動 ①成功する ②(〜の)跡を継ぐ **succeed in doing** 〜する事に成功する
- **success** 名 成功、幸運、上首尾
- **successful** 形 成功した、うまくいった
- **successfully** 副 首尾よく、うまく
- **succession** 名 連続、相続、継承
- **such a** そのような
- **such as** たとえば〜、〜のような
- **sue** 動 訴える、訴訟する
- **suffer** 動 ①(苦痛・損害などを)受ける、こうむる ②(病気に)なる、苦しむ、悩む
- **suggest** 動 ①提案する ②示唆する

- **suggestion** 名 ①提案, 忠告 ②気配, 暗示
- **sum** 名 ①総計 ②金額
- **summertime** 名 夏季, 夏時間
- **summit** 名 ①頂上, 頂点 ②《the -》首脳会議, サミット
- **sunk** 動 sink (沈む) の過去分詞
- **superior** 形 優れた, 優秀な, 上方の
- **superpower** 名 超大国, 強国, 異常な力
- **supply** 動 供給[配給]する, 補充する
- **support** 動 ①支える, 支持する ②養う, 援助する 名 ①支え, 支持 ②援助, 扶養
- **supporter** 名 後援者, 支持者, サポーター, 支柱
- **suppress** 動 ①抑える, 抑圧する ②隠す ③我慢する
- **supreme** 形 最高の, 究極の
- **Supreme Commander** 最高司令官, 総司令官
- **Supreme Court** 合衆国最高裁判所《アメリカ合衆国の最上級の裁判所であり, 連邦政府の司法府 (連邦裁判所) を統括している》
- **surface** 名 ①表面, 水面 ②うわべ, 外見 **on the surface** 外面は, うわべは
- **surprise** 熟 **to one's surprise** ~が驚いたことに
- **surprised** 形 驚いた
- **surrender** 名 降伏, 降参, 明け渡し 動 降伏する, 引き渡す
- **survey** 名 ①概観 ②調査
- **survive** 動 ①生き残る, 存続する, なんとかなる ②長生きする, 切り抜ける
- **suspect** 動 疑う, (~ではないかと) 思う
- **Swede** 名 スウェーデン人
- **Switzerland** 名 スイス《国名》
- **sworn** 動 swear (誓う) の過去分詞 **sworn enemy** 目の敵
- **symbol** 名 シンボル, 象徴
- **symbolic** 形 象徴する, 象徴的な

T

- **tactics** 名 戦術, 兵法
- **Taft-Hartley Act** タフト＝ハートリー法《労働組合の活動と勢力を監視する米国連邦法, 1947年労使関係法の通称》
- **take advantage of** ~を利用する, ~につけ込む
- **take control of** ~を制御[管理]する, 支配する
- **take on** ~に立ち向かう
- **take over** 引き継ぐ, 支配する, 乗っ取る
- **take part in** ~に参加する
- **take up** 取り上げる, 拾い上げる, やり始める
- **talented** 形 才能のある, 有能な
- **tax** 名 ①税 ②重荷, 重い負担 動 ①課税する ②重荷を負わせる
- **Tax Reform Act of 1964** 1964年税制改革法《1964年2月26日にリンドン・ジョンソン大統領が署名した超党派の減税法案。個人所得税減税に加えて, 法人税率をわずかに下げ, 最低基準控除を導入した》
- **taxation** 名 課税, 徴税
- **Taylor** 名 ザカリー・テイラー《第12代アメリカ合衆国大統領 (任期1849-1850), 陸軍少将》
- **technological** 名 技術上の, (科学) 技術の
- **technology** 名 テクノロジー, 科学技術
- **telegraph** 名 電報, 電信
- **television** 名 テレビ

A Short History of America

- **temporary** 形 一時的な, 仮の
- **Tennessee** 名 テネシー州
- **tension** 名 緊張(関係), ぴんと張ること
- **tension-filled** 形 厳しく張り詰めた
- **term** 名 ①期間, 期限 ②語, 用語 ③《-s》条件 ④《-s》関係, 仲
- **terribly** 副 ひどく
- **territory** 名 ①領土 ②(広い)地域, 範囲, 領域
- **Territory of New Mexico** ニューメキシコ準州
- **terrorism** 名 テロ行為, 暴力行為
- **terrorist** 名 テロリスト
- **testing** 名 テストすること
- **Texan** 形 テキサス州の
- **Texas** 名 テキサス州
- **thanks to** ～のおかげで, ～の結果
- **Thanksgiving** 名 感謝祭
- **Theodore Roosevelt** セオドア・ルーズベルト《第26代アメリカ合衆国大統領(任期1901–1909)》
- **therefore** 副 したがって, それゆえ, その結果
- **thinking** 名 考えること, 思考
- **38th parallel** 北緯38度線《第二次世界大戦末期に朝鮮半島を横切る北緯38度線に引かれたアメリカ軍とソ連軍の分割占領ライン》
- **Thomas Edison** トーマス・エジソン《アメリカ合衆国の発明家, 起業家(1847–1931)》
- **Thomas Gage** トマス・ゲイジ《イギリスの将軍。1763年から1775年まで, 特にアメリカ独立戦争の初期に北アメリカの最高司令官だった(1719–1787)》
- **Thomas Jefferson** トーマス・ジェファーソン《第3代アメリカ合衆国大統領(任期1801–1809)》
- **Thomas Paine** トマス・ペイン《イギリス出身のアメリカ合衆国の哲学者, 政治活動家(1737–1809)》
- **those who** ～する人々
- **though** 接 ①～にもかかわらず, ～だが ②たとえ～でも 副 しかし **even though** ～であるけれども, ～にもかかわらず
- **thousands of** 何千という
- **threat** 名 おどし, 脅迫
- **threaten** 動 脅かす, おびやかす, 脅迫する
- **throughout** 前 ①～中, ～を通じて ②～のいたるところに
- **thrown out of** ～から追い出される
- **thus** 副 ①このように ②これだけ ③かくて, だから
- **tight** 形 堅い, きつい, ぴんと張った
- **tighten** 動 ①ぴんと張る, 堅く締める ②余裕がなくなる ③厳しくなる
- **time** 名 **a hard time** つらい時期 **at that time** その時 **at the same time as** ～と同時に **at this time** 現時点では, このとき **by this time** この時までに, もうすでに **in time** 間に合って, やがて
- **tip** 名 先端, 頂点
- **tobacco** 名 たばこ
- **topic** 名 話題, 見出し
- **total** 形 合計の, 全体の, 完全な 名 全体, 合計 動 合計する
- **tough** 形 堅い, 丈夫な, たくましい, 骨の折れる, 困難な
- **Townshend Acts** タウンゼンド諸法《イギリス帝国の議会が1767年以降に成立させた, 英領アメリカの植民地に関する一連の法令》
- **trade** 名 取引, 貿易, 商業 動 取引する, 貿易する, 商売する
- **trader** 名 ①商人, 貿易業者 ②投機家
- **traditional** 形 伝統的な

Word List

- **traffic** 名 通行, 往来, 交通(量), 貿易
- **tragic** 形 悲劇の, 痛ましい
- **trail** 名 (通った)跡
- **transatlantic** 形 大西洋横断の
- **transcontinental** 形 大陸横断の
- **transcontinental railroad** 大陸横断鉄道
- **transportation** 名 交通(機関), 輸送手段
- **treason** 名 裏切り[反逆]行為, 背信
- **treasury** 名 ①宝庫, 国庫 ②《the T-》財務省, 大蔵省
- **treat** 動 扱う
- **treaty** 名 条約, 協定
- **Treaty of Ghent** ガン条約《米英戦争の講和条約で, 1814年12月に南ネーデルラント(ベルギー)のヘント(ガン)で結ばれた》
- **Treaty of Guadalupe Hidalgo** グアダルーペ・イダルゴ条約《米墨戦争(1846-1848)を終結させた1848年5月の条約》
- **Treaty of Versailles** ヴェルサイユ条約《1919年6月28日にフランスのヴェルサイユで調印された, 第一次世界大戦における連合国とドイツの間で締結された講和条約の総称》
- **Trenton** 名 トレントン(ニュージャージー州)《都市名》
- **trial** 名 裁判
- **tribe** 名 部族, 一族
- **tried** 形 試験済みの, 信頼できる
- **troop** 名 群れ, 隊
- **tropical** 形 熱帯の
- **true** 熟 come true 実現する
- **truly** 副 ①全く, 本当に, 真に ②心から, 誠実に
- **trust** 名 ①信用, 信頼, 委託 ②企業合同, トラスト
- **trusteeship** 名 信託統治

- **Trusteeship Council** 国際連合信託統治理事会《国際連合の主要機関の一つ》
- **turbulence** 名 大荒れ, 騒乱, 乱気流
- **turn to** 〜を始める, 〜に頼る
- **typical** 形 典型的な, 象徴的な
- **tyranny** 名 専制政治, 暴政, 残虐

U

- **Ulysses S. Grant** ユリシーズ・グラント《アメリカ合衆国の軍人, 政治家。南北戦争時の北軍の将軍および第18代アメリカ合衆国大統領(任期1869–1877)》
- **unable** 形 《be – to 〜》〜することができない
- **unanimous** 形 (全員が)同意見の, 満場一致の
- **Uncle Tom's Cabin** 『アンクル・トムの小屋』《アメリカ合衆国のストウ夫人(ハリエット・ビーチャー・ストウ)の小説(1852)》
- **unconditional** 形 無条件の, 絶対的な
- **unconstitutional** 形 憲法に違反する, 違憲の
- **uncultivated** 形 耕作[開墾]されていない
- **underground** 形 地下の[にある] 名 地下鉄, 地下(道)
- **undertake** 動 ①引き受ける ②始める, 企てる
- **unemployment** 名 失業(状態)
- **unethical** 形 非倫理的な, 非道徳的な
- **unfair** 形 不公平な, 不当な
- **unfortunate** 形 不運な, あいにくな, 不適切な
- **unfortunately** 副 不幸にも, 運悪く

A Short History of America

- **union** 名 ①結合, 合併, 融合 ②連合国家
- **Union of States** アメリカ合衆国《アメリカ連合規約（1777年採択, 1781年施行）によって規定された13の邦からなる連合国家》
- **Union Pacific Railroad** ユニオン・パシフィック鉄道《アメリカ合衆国最大規模の鉄道会社》
- **unique** 形 唯一の, ユニークな, 独自の
- **unite** 動 ①1つにする［なる］, 合わせる, 結ぶ ②結束する, 団結する
- **united** 形 団結した, まとまった, 連合した
- **United Kingdom** 名 連合王国, 英国, イギリス《国》
- **United Nations** 名《the –》国際連合（= U.N./UN）
- **United Nations Charter** 国際連合憲章《国際連合の設立根拠となる条約》
- **United States Air Force** アメリカ空軍
- **United States of America** アメリカ合衆国
- **United States Weather Bureau** アメリカ国立気象局
- **unknown** 形 知られていない, 不明の
- **unofficial** 形 非公式［公認］の
- **unpopular** 形 人気がない, はやらない
- **unprecedented** 形 前例［先例］のない
- **unsuccessful** 形 失敗の, 不成功の
- **up and down** 上がったり下がったり, 行ったり来たり, あちこちと
- **uprising** 名 反乱, 暴動, 謀反
- **upset** 形 憤慨して, 動揺して 動 気を悪くさせる, (心・神経など)をかき乱す
- **urban** 形 都会の, 都市の

- **urge** 動 ①せき立てる, 強力に推し進める, かりたてる ②《- … to ～》に～するよう熱心に勧める
- **use** 熟 in use 使用されて
- **used** 動 ①use（使う）の過去, 過去分詞 ②《– to》よく～したものだ, 以前は～であった 形 慣れている, 《get [become] – to》～に慣れてくる
- **USS** 略 アメリカ海軍艦船の艦船接頭辞《United States Ship の略》
- **USS Constitution** コンスティチューション《アメリカ海軍の木造船殻, 3本マスト, 砲数44門のフリゲート。愛称オールド・アイアンサイズ》
- **USS West Virginia** ウェストバージニア《アメリカ海軍の戦艦。1941年12月8日の大日本帝国海軍による真珠湾攻撃を受けた》
- **Utah** 名 ユタ州
- **utility** 名 ①実用性 ②《-ties》公共サービス《ガス, 電気, 水道など》

V

- **valid** 形 ①有効な ②正当な, 妥当な
- **valley** 名 谷, 谷間
- **Valley Forge** バレーフォージ《アメリカ独立戦争中の1777年から1778年にかけての冬, 大陸軍が宿営地としたペンシルベニア州にある場所》
- **value** 動 評価する, 値をつける, 大切にする
- **variety** 名 ①変化, 多様性, 寄せ集め ②種類
- **various** 形 変化に富んだ, さまざまの, たくさんの
- **Vasco Núñez de Balboa** バスコ・ヌーニェス・デ・バルバ《スペインの探検家・植民地政治家。ヨーロッパ人として初めて太平洋に到達した（1475-1519）》
- **vast** 形 広大な, 巨大な, ばく大な

Word List

- **venture** 名 冒険(的事業), 危険
- **Vera Cruz** ベラクルス州(メキシコ)
- **Vermont** 名 バーモント州
- **via** 前 ～経由で, ～によって
- **vice** 形 代理の
- **Vice President** 副大統領
- **vicious** 形 悪意のある, 意地の悪い, 扱いにくい vicious circle 悪循環
- **victim** 名 犠牲者, 被害者
- **victorious** 形 勝利を得た, 勝った
- **victory** 名 勝利, 優勝
- **Viet Cong** 名 南ベトナム解放民族戦線《南ベトナムで1960年12月に結成された反サイゴン政権・アメリカ・反帝国主義を標榜する統一戦線組織》
- **Vietnam** 名 ベトナム《国名》
- **Vietnam War** ベトナム戦争《インドシナ戦争後に南北に分裂したベトナムで発生した戦争の総称》
- **Vietnamese** 形 ベトナム(人)の
- **view** 熟 point of view 考え方, 視点
- **violence** 名 ①暴力, 乱暴 ②激しさ
- **violent** 形 暴力的な, 激しい
- **Virginia** 名 バージニア州
- **Virginia Assembly** バージニア植民地議会
- **Virginia House of Burgesses** バージニア植民地立法府下院《1619年にジェームズタウンで開催されたアメリカで最初の議会》
- **Virginian** 名 バージニア人
- **Virginian Army** 北バージニア軍《南北戦争東部戦線において南軍の主力となって戦った軍》
- **visible** 形 目に見える, 明らかな
- **vision** 名 ①視力 ②先見, 洞察力
- **volunteer** 名 志願者, ボランティア volunteer soldier 志願兵, 義勇兵
- **vote** 名 投票(権), 票決 動 投票する, 投票して決める
- **voter** 名 投票者
- **voting** 形 投票の
- **voyage** 名 航海

W

- **wage** 名 賃金, 給料
- **wagon** 名 荷馬車
- **Wall St.** ウォール街《ニューヨーク市マンハッタンの南端部(ロウアーマンハッタン)に位置する細いストリートの一つ》
- **Walter Raleigh, Sir** ウォルター・ローリー《イングランドの廷臣, 探検家。新世界における最初のイングランド植民地を築いた(1552または1554–1618)》
- **war** 熟 civil war 内戦, 内乱
- **War of 1812** 米英戦争《1812年6月から1815年2月までの期間にイギリス, その植民地であるカナダ及びイギリスと同盟を結んだインディアン諸部族とアメリカ合衆国との間でおこなわれた戦争》
- **War of Spanish Succession** スペイン継承戦争《18世紀初めにスペイン王位の継承者を巡ってヨーロッパ諸国間で行われた戦争(1701–1714)》
- **warehouse** 名 倉庫, 問屋, 商品保管所
- **warfare** 名 戦争, 交戦状態, 戦闘行為
- **warming** 名 暖めること, 暖まること, 温度上昇
- **warship** 名 軍艦
- **wartime** 名 戦時(中) 形 戦時の
- **Washington D.C.** ワシントンD.C.
- **Washington, state of** ワシントン州

A Short History of America

- **Watergate scandal** ウォーターゲート事件《1972年6月17日にワシントンD.C.の民主党本部で起きた盗聴侵入事件に始まったアメリカの政治スキャンダル》
- **wave** 名 波
- **way** 熟 in this way このようにして　on one's way to ～に行く途中で　one's way (to ～) (～への)途中で　way of ～する方法　way of life 生き様, 生き方, 暮らし方
- **weaken** 動 弱くなる, 弱める
- **wealthy** 形 裕福な, 金持ちの
- **weapon** 名 武器, 兵器
- **well** 熟 as well なお, その上, 同様に　as well as ～と同様に　be well-ed よく[十分に]～された
- **Wendell L. Willkie** ウェンデル・L・ウィルキー《アメリカの政治家, 弁護士。1940年の共和党大統領候補 (1892-1944)》
- **Wesleyan Female College** ウェスレヤン大学《ジョージア州メイコンの大学》
- **West Berlin** 西ベルリン《第二次世界大戦終戦後1949年から1990年まで, アメリカ・イギリス・フランスが占領したベルリン西部の地域》
- **West Coast** ウェストコースト, 米国の西海岸
- **West Germany** 西ドイツ《1949年5月23日から1990年10月2日までのドイツ連邦共和国の通称》
- **West Indies** 西インド諸島《中米の諸島》
- **western** 形 ①西の, 西側の ②《W-》西洋の
- **whether** 接 ～かどうか, ～かまたは…, ～であろうとなかろうと
- **Whig Party** ホイッグ党《アメリカ合衆国にかつて存在した政党 (1833-1860)》
- **who** 熟 those who ～する人々
- **whole** 名《the -》全体, 全部
- **wholly** 副 完全に, すっかり
- **whom** 代 ①誰を[に] ②《関係代名詞》～するところの人, そしてその人を
- **widen** 動 広くなる[する], 大きく開く
- **widespread** 形 広範囲におよぶ, 広く知られた
- **wilderness** 名 荒野, 荒れ地
- **Wiley Post** ウィリー・ポスト《アメリカ合衆国の飛行家。世界一周飛行などで有名になった (1898-1935)》
- **William Harris Crawford** ウィリアム・ハリス・クロウフォード《アメリカ合衆国の政治家。1824年の大統領選挙では民主共和党の大統領候補 (1772-1834)》
- **William Harrison** ウィリアム・ハリソン《第9代アメリカ合衆国大統領 (任期1841-1841)》
- **William McKinley** ウィリアム・マッキンリー《第25代アメリカ合衆国大統領 (任期1897-1901)》
- **William Penn** ウィリアム・ペン《イギリスの植民地だった現在のアメリカ合衆国にフィラデルフィア市を建設しペンシルベニア州を整備した (1644-1718)》
- **windmill** 名 風車
- **Winfield Scott** ウィンフィールド・スコット《アメリカ陸軍の将軍, 外交官 (1786-1866)》
- **winner** 名 勝利者, 成功者
- **winning** 名 勝つこと, 勝利,《-s》賞金
- **Wisconsin** 名 ウィスコンシン州
- **Wisconsin Territory** ウィスコンシン準州
- **withdraw** 動 引っ込める, 取り下げる, (預金を)引き出す
- **withdrew** 動 withdraw (引っ込める)の過去

Word List

- **within** 前 ①～の中[内]に、～の内部に ②～以内で、～を越えないで
- **Women's Army Corps** 婦人陸軍部隊《第二次世界大戦中のアメリカ合衆国において、アメリカ陸軍の補助部隊として1942年5月14日に設立・編成された組織》
- **wooden** 形 木製の、木でできた
- **Woodrow Wilson** ウッドロウ・ウィルソン《第28代アメリカ合衆国大統領(任期1913-1921)》
- **word** 熟 in other words すなわち、言い換えれば
- **work on** ～で働く
- **worker** 名 仕事をする人、労働者
- **world** 熟 all over the world 世界中に
- **world affairs** 世界情勢
- **World Trade Center** ワールドトレードセンター《かつてアメリカ合衆国のニューヨーク市マンハッタン区のローワー・マンハッタンに位置していた商業施設。2001年の9月11日に発生した、アメリカ同時多発テロ事件の標的となった》
- **World War I** 第一次世界大戦《1914年7月28日から1918年11月11日にかけて、連合国対中央同盟国の戦闘により繰り広げられた世界大戦》
- **World War II** 第二次世界大戦《1939年から1945年までの6年間、ドイツ、日本、イタリアの日独伊三国同盟を中心とする枢軸国陣営と、イギリス、ソビエト連邦、アメリカ、中華民国などの連合国陣営との間で戦われた全世界的規模の巨大戦争》
- **worldwide** 形 世界的な、世界中に広まった、世界規模の
- **worried** 形 心配そうな、不安げな
- **worse** 形 いっそう悪い、より劣った、よりひどい 副 いっそう悪く
- **worsen** 動 悪化する[させる]
- **worst** 形《the-》最も悪い、いちばんひどい
- **worthless** 形 価値のない、役立たずの
- **wound** 動 ①負傷させる、(感情を)害する ②wind (巻く)の過去、過去分詞
- **Wounded Knee Massacre** ウンデット・ニーの虐殺《1890年12月29日、サウスダコタ州ウーンデッド・ニーで、ミネコンジュー他のスー族インディアンのバンド(集団)に対して、米軍の第7騎兵隊が行った民族浄化》
- **Wright brothers** ライト兄弟《アメリカ出身の動力飛行機の発明者。1903年に世界初の有人動力飛行に成功した》
- **wrongly** 副 誤って、間違って
- **Wyoming** 名 ワイオミング州

Y

- **Yalta Conference** ヤルタ会談《1945年2月4日から11日にかけて、当時のソ連クリミア自治ソビエト社会主義共和国のヤルタ近郊のリヴァディア宮殿で行われた、アメリカ合衆国・イギリス・ソビエト連邦による首脳会談》
- **year** 熟 for years 何年も for ~ years ～年間、～年にわたって
- **yet to** いまだ～されない

Z

- **Zenger trial** ゼンガーの裁判《ニューヨーク植民地でドイツ系アメリカ植民地人ジョン・ピーター・ゼンガーが植民地総督を批判する新聞を発行したことで逮捕・訴追されたが、陪審の無罪評決を受けた》
- **zone** 名 地帯、区域

English Conversational Ability Test
国際英語会話能力検定

● E-CATとは…
英語が話せるようになるための
テストです。インターネット
ベースで、30分であなたの発
話力をチェックします。

www.ecatexam.com

● iTEP®とは…
世界各国の企業、政府機関、アメリカの大学
300校以上が、英語能力判定テストとして採用。
オンラインによる90分のテストで文法、リー
ディング、リスニング、ライティング、スピー
キングの5技能をスコア化。iTEP®は、留学、就
職、海外赴任などに必要な、世界に通用する英
語力を総合的に評価する画期的なテストです。

www.itepexamjapan.com

ラダーシリーズ
A Short History of America アメリカ史

2019年1月11日　第1刷発行
2023年4月6日　第3刷発行

著　者　西海コエン

発行者　浦　　晋亮

発行所　IBCパブリッシング株式会社
　　　　〒162-0804 東京都新宿区中里町29番3号
　　　　菱秀神楽坂ビル
　　　　Tel. 03-3513-4511　Fax. 03-3513-4512
　　　　www.ibcpub.co.jp

© IBC Publishing, Inc. 2019

印刷　株式会社シナノパブリッシングプレス
装丁　伊藤 理恵
組版データ　Minion Pro Regular + Myriad Pro Bold

落丁本・乱丁本は、小社宛にお送りください。送料小社負担にてお取り替えいたし
ます。本書の無断複写(コピー)は著作権法上での例外を除き禁じられています。

Printed in Japan
ISBN978-4-7946-0569-6